Manchester guide 2024

Your Essential Companion Featuring Up-to-Date Information, Photos, and Maps

By

Lawrence Allison

Copyright © 2024 by Lawrence Allison

All rights reserved. No part of this publication may be reproduced, distributed, or transmitted in any form or by any means, including photocopying, recording, or other electronic or mechanical methods, without the prior written permission of the publisher, except in the case of brief quotations embodied in critical reviews and certain other noncommercial uses permitted by copyright law.

Table of contents

Introduction..7
   Maps... 12
   Welcome to Manchester.................................. 15
   Overview of Manchester..................................22
      Historical Significance...............................23
      Cultural Diversity and Vibrancy.........................23
      Modern Architecture and Urban Development. 25
      Learning and Creativity......................................26
      Recreation and Green Areas.............................26
      Culinary Excellence... 27
      Connectivity and Accessibility...........................28
   How to Use This Guide...................................29

Chapter 1: Getting to Manchester.............................36
   Transportation Options................................... 36
   Navigating the City...44
      Recognising Manchester's Architecture............45
      Accredited Taxi Companies............................... 51
      Parking and Road Safety Advice...................... 52

Chapter 2: Top Attractions.. 54
   The Lowry.. 55
   Historical Sites... 65
      Manchester Cathedral....................................... 68
      The Whitworth...69
      Castlefield.. 70
   Museums and Galleries................................... 75
      Manchester Museum.. 76

The Whitworth..77
　　　Manchester Art Gallery......................................77
　　　Museum of Science and Industry.....................79
　　　North of the Imperial War Museum..................80
　　　HOUSE Manchester..81
　　　Science and Industry Museum.........................81
　Parks and Outdoor Spaces......................................83
　　　Park Heaton..84
　　　Whitworth Park...86
Chapter 3: Culinary Experiences............................. 93
　Must-Try Dishes..93
　　　Customary British Cuisine................................ 93
　　　Wide Range of Foreign Cuisines.......................95
　　　Fusion and Modern British Cooking..................97
　　　Modern British Dishes at Australasia................97
　　　Desserts and Sweet Treats...............................99
　　　Markets and Street Cuisine............................ 101
　Popular Restaurants and Cafés............................103
　Food Markets and Street Food............................ 114
　　　Food Markets in the Northern Quarter........... 117
　　　Events and Festivals of Street Food............... 118
　　　Advice for Savouring Street Food and Food Markets in Manchester....................................119
Chapter 4: Cultural Insights..................................... 122
　Local Customs and Traditions.............................. 122
　　　Amicable Mancunian Essence........................122
　　　Football Enthusiasm.. 123
　　　Vast Musical Legacy.. 124
　　　Bars and Conversation.................................... 125

Festivals & Events.. 125
Conventional Marketplaces........................... 127
Honouring Our Heritage................................127
Honouring Regional Customs......................... 128
Festivals and Events...130
Manchester International Festival.................. 130
Pride in Manchester.. 131
Food and Drink Festival in Manchester.......... 132
Street Art Festival Darnell.............................. 133
Winter Wonderland with Christmas Markets...134
Manchester Running Events & Marathon....... 135
Art and Music Scene...137
A Renowned Musical Heritage....................... 137
Symbolic Music Locations.............................. 138
Vibrant Creative Spaces and Art Galleries..... 139
The Role of Education and Institutions........... 141
Advice for Appreciating Music and Art in Manchester... 143

Chapter 5: Essential Tips and Laws....................... 145
Important Travel Tips... 145
Currency and Payments................................. 145
Travel Advice.. 146
Security and Safety...147
Spoken Word and Verbal Exchange............... 148
Atmosphere and Apparel................................ 148
Reservations for Lodging............................... 149
Regional Traditions and Protocols.................. 149
Emergency Numbers and Medical Information..... 150

5

>   Internet and connectivity................................. 150
>   Visitor Information Desks............................... 151
>   Usability.. 151
>   Packing List Essentials................................. 152
> Safety and Health Information.............................. 153
>   Overall Safety Advice..................................... 154
>   Contacts for Emergencies............................. 155
>   Medical Institutions.. 156
>   Insurance for Travel....................................... 157
>   COVID-19 and Health Care for All.................. 158
>   Municipal Rules and Laws.............................. 159
>   Usability.. 159
>   Maintaining Your Health................................. 160
> Local Laws and Regulations................................. 162
>   Drinking Alcohol... 163
>   Smoking Laws.. 164
>   Laws Concerning Drugs................................. 164
>   Disorder and Public Behaviour....................... 165
>   Road and Traffic Laws.................................... 166
>   Honouring Regional Traditions and Etiquette. 167
>   Emergency Support and Services.................. 168
> **Conclusion**.. 170
> **Bonus Section**... 183

Introduction

Welcome to Manchester, a city with a rich cultural tapestry that combines cutting-edge innovation and industrial legacy to create an environment unmatched by any other. Whether you're a history buff, a music lover, a sports enthusiast, or simply seeking to see one of the UK's most dynamic cities, Manchester guarantees an amazing experience. As your indispensable companion, this guide is packed with up-to-date information, breathtaking images, and thorough maps to help you navigate and relish every moment of your visit between 2024 and 2025.

A Quick Tour Across Time

Manchester's tale is one of resiliency and change. The city's famous mills and industries, which were once the centre of the Industrial Revolution, sparked unheard-of expansion and creativity. These historic locations now mix with contemporary buildings and bustling neighbourhoods, illustrating a city that embraces the future while paying tribute to its history. Manchester skilfully combines the old and the new, as evidenced by the magnificent architecture of the Manchester Town Hall and the modern charm of MediaCityUK.

Cultural Fusion Centre

Manchester is home to many different communities that add to its lively social fabric, making it a true cultural mosaic. In addition to a vibrant artistic scene and a number of events, this diversity is honoured through delicious food. The city features world-class museums like the Museum of Science and Industry and the Manchester Art Gallery, alongside cutting-edge galleries and theaters that showcase both local and international talent. Manchester's storied music scene, which gave rise to great bands like Oasis, The Smiths, and Joy Division, will delight music lovers.

Traditions and Faith

A major part of Manchester's cultural fabric is religion. The diverse population of the city is reflected in the multitude of faiths that call it home. From the towering Manchester Cathedral, with its stunning Gothic architecture, to vibrant mosques, temples, and churches, tourists will find places of worship that appeal to varied spiritual requirements. The multiplicity of religions in the city enhances its social and cultural life by promoting an atmosphere of tolerance and respect for one another.

Useful Advice: Money and Laws

Comprehending the pragmatic facets of travelling to Manchester guarantees a seamless and delightful journey. The currency in Manchester is the British Pound Sterling (£). Although most places accept credit cards and there are plenty of ATMs, it is always a good idea to keep extra cash on hand for smaller markets or sellers.

Manchester abides by laws and regulations that are applicable to the entire United Kingdom. It is important for visitors to be informed about all local rules, such as those pertaining to transportation, public smoking bans, and alcohol usage. Although the city has a warm and inviting reputation, it is crucial to abide by local laws and customs to make sure that everyone has a good time while there.

Capturing the Spirit of Manchester

The allure of Manchester is that it has something to offer everyone. Manchester encourages you to design your own special experiences, whether you are strolling around the vibrant Northern Quarter with its oddball shops and street art, taking in a game at the iconic Old Trafford Stadium, or unwinding in one of the numerous parks in the city, including Heaton Park. The city's well-functioning public transport system makes it simple to discover every aspect, from the hip neighbourhoods to the tranquil suburbs.

Let this guide be your reliable travel buddy as you go off on your Manchester journey. Explore undiscovered treasures, confidently arrange your schedule, and fully engage in Manchester's lively culture all of which make this city a must-see. Get ready to be enthralled by the warmth, inventiveness, and vitality that characterise this extraordinary city. Greetings from Manchester, where each visit is an opportunity to tell a tale.

Maps

Manchester

How to Scan QR code
1. Open the Camera App
2. Point Your Camera at the QR Code
3. Wait for the Notification to Appear
4. Tap the Notification Banner
5. Access the Linked Content
6. Close the Camera App

12

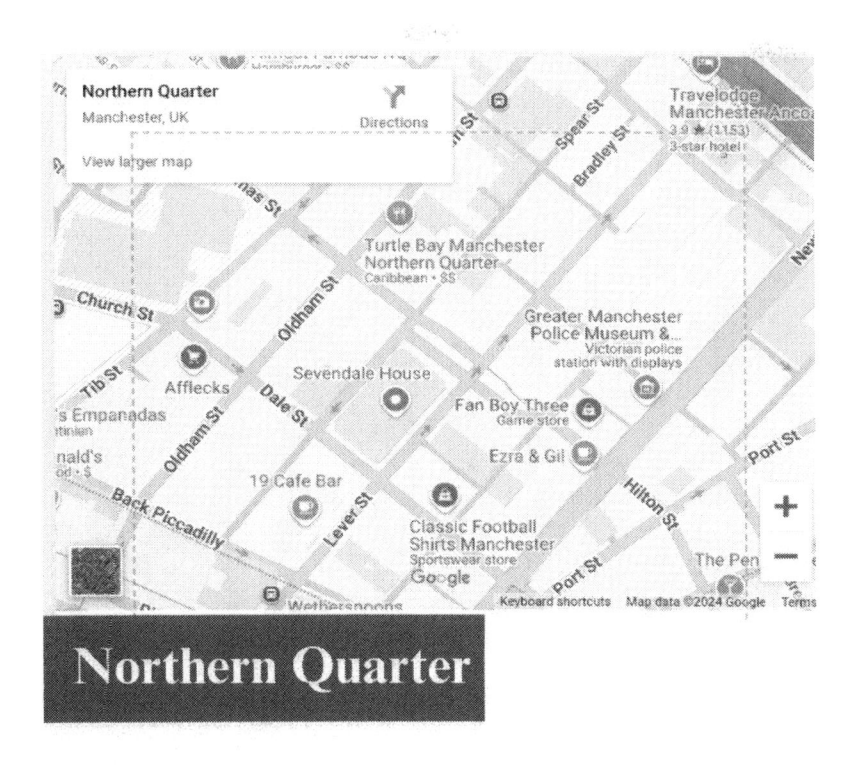

Northern Quarter

How to Scan QR code

1. Open the Camera App
2. Point Your Camera at the QR Code
3. Wait for the Notification to Appear
4. Tap the Notification Banner
5. Access the Linked Content
6. Close the Camera App

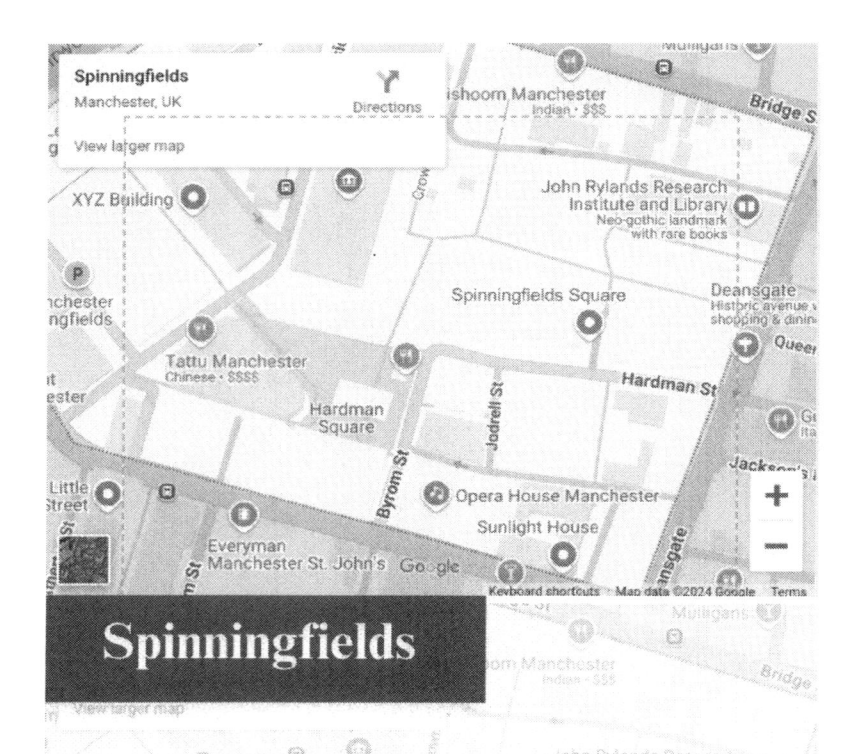

Spinningfields

How to Scan QR code

1. Open the Camera App
2. Point Your Camera at the QR Code
3. Wait for the Notification to Appear
4. Tap the Notification Banner
5. Access the Linked Content
6. Close the Camera App

Welcome to Manchester

Located in the centre of Northern England, Manchester is a bustling and energetic metropolis. Manchester, a city renowned for its innovative culture, industrial past, and friendly demeanour, is an example of perseverance and ingenuity. This guide is your indispensable travel companion, including up-to-date information, gorgeous images, and thorough maps to make sure your trip between 2024 and 2025 is nothing short of extraordinary whether you are visiting for the first time or coming back to discover more of its hidden jewels.

A Harmonious City of Contrasts

Manchester skilfully combines the old and the new to create a distinctive skyline that combines modern and historic structures. As you go around the city, you will see slick glass skyscrapers in the city centre amid grand Victorian buildings like Manchester Town Hall and the stunning neo-Gothic Manchester Cathedral. This tasteful contrast serves as a visual metaphor for Manchester's capacity to embrace the future while paying tribute to its history.

Cultural Epicentre

Manchester is a major hub for culture, with a flourishing and diverse arts sector. World-class organisations can be found in the city, including the Whitworth Art Gallery, which is well-known for its exhibitions of historical and contemporary art, and the Manchester Museum, which has an amazing collection of artefacts from all over the world. Theatre lovers can enjoy a variety of shows at the Royal Exchange Theatre and HOME Manchester, including avant-garde productions and classic plays.

With its rich musical heritage as the birthplace of iconic bands like The Smiths, Oasis, and Joy Division, Manchester is a music lover's dream come true. From cosy bars to massive concert halls, the city is still teeming with live music places, so there is always something exciting going on for fans of all genres.

Recreation and Sports

An important part of Manchester's identity is its sports culture. The city is home to Manchester United and Manchester City, two of the most well-known football teams in the world, each with an ardent fan base and cutting-edge venues, Old Trafford and the Etihad Stadium, respectively. Even if you are not a huge football fan, going to a game or seeing these historic locations provides an exciting window into the local way of life.

Beyond football, Manchester provides a number of leisure activities. Large green areas like Heaton Park and Fletcher Moss Botanical Garden offer tranquil getaways from the bustle of the city. The adjacent Peak District provides chances for hiking, cycling, and scenic landscape exploration for people looking for adventure.

Savoury Treats

The variety of Manchester's population is reflected in its culinary scene. The city offers everything for every taste, from cosmopolitan eateries featuring flavours from around the world to classic British pubs serving hearty meals. Do not miss Rusholme's colourful Curry Mile, which is well-known for its real South Asian food, or the hip Northern Quarter, which is home to a variety of independent cafes, artisanal bakeries, and cutting-edge restaurants.

You may try a range of foods in one location at street food markets like Mackie Mayor and the Arndale Market, which provide a diverse selection of alternatives for a leisurely dinner or a quick bite. Manchester's food culture offers something to suit every need, be it gourmet street tacos, vegan delicacies, or a traditional Sunday roast.

Effective Transit

Manchester's extensive transport system makes getting around easy. Transport for Greater Manchester (TfGM) runs a comprehensive bus and tram network in the city, which makes it simple to go to all part of the city. Manchester Airport acts as a significant international gateway, while Manchester Piccadilly Station links you to important destinations throughout the United Kingdom for longer trips.

The city's expanding network of bike lanes and rental programs, which encourage environmentally friendly travel options, will be appreciated by cyclists. Furthermore, Manchester is a walking city with a lot of nearby attractions, so you can explore on foot and take your time discovering quaint streets, secret courtyards, and lively neighbourhoods.

Modifications to Fit Any Budget

Manchester provides a variety of lodging options to fit every taste and budget, whether you are looking for opulent hotels, quaint bed and breakfasts, or affordable hostels. You can choose a convenient and comfortable location to stay, from the sleek suites of the Midland Hotel to the contemporary comforts of the Hilton Manchester Deansgate.

Choose to stay in one of the city's distinctive boutique hotels or serviced apartments for a more authentic local experience; they offer a stylish yet functional combination. Regardless of where you choose to stay, you'll be well-positioned to discover all that Manchester has to offer.

Spread the Manchester ethos

The people of Manchester are what really make the city charming; they are the amiable, varied, and imaginative people that make it a pleasant and motivating place to visit. With its vibrant environment ranging from bustling markets and exciting nightlife to serene parks and historical sites, Manchester welcomes you to immerse yourself and make lifelong memories.

Let this guide be your reliable travel buddy as you go off on your Manchester journey. With the help of our breathtaking images, detailed maps, and up-to-date information, explore the city's top attractions, unearth hidden gems, and travel around with ease. Greetings from Manchester, where each visit opens a new chapter in your journey.

Overview of Manchester

Manchester, often hailed as the cultural and economic powerhouse of Northern England, is a city that seamlessly blends its rich industrial past with a vibrant, forward-thinking present. As one of the United Kingdom's most dynamic cities, Manchester offers visitors a diverse array of experiences, from historic landmarks and world-class museums to cutting-edge architecture and a thriving nightlife. This overview provides a snapshot of what makes Manchester a must-visit destination for travelers in 2024 and beyond.

Historical Significance

Manchester has a rich history dating back to the Industrial Revolution, and because of its crucial position in the world's textile industry, the city has been dubbed "Cottonopolis." The city's industrial legacy is still visible today in its impressive architecture and heritage sites. Visitors can get a glimpse into Manchester's revolutionary past by visiting landmarks like the Science and Industry Museum, which documents the city's technological advancements, and the stunning neo-Gothic Manchester Town Hall. In addition, the abandoned factories and canals have been transformed into hip restaurants, bars, and cultural centres, maintaining the city's legacy while promoting contemporary creativity.

Cultural Diversity and Vibrancy

Manchester is well known for its diverse population, which is evident in its festivals, restaurants, and residential areas. The city's diverse population contributes to its lively and welcoming environment. Visitors can explore the busy Chinatown, one of the largest in Europe, offering a wealth of authentic Asian cuisines and cultural activities. Due to the diverse population, there are numerous cultural festivals held all year long that celebrate everything from food and art to music and film.

Manchester has an incredibly active cultural culture, with lots of theatres, galleries, and live music venues. The Manchester Art Gallery houses an extensive collection of artworks spanning centuries, while contemporary spaces like HOME Manchester showcase innovative performances and exhibitions. The city's music heritage is legendary, having birthed influential bands such as The Smiths, Oasis, and Joy Division. Today, Manchester continues to be a hub for live music, with venues like the Manchester Arena and the O2 Ritz hosting both local talents and international stars.

Modern Architecture and Urban Development

Manchester's skyline is a testament to its blend of historic and modern architecture. The city has undergone significant urban development in recent years, with projects like the Beetham Tower and the renovation of the Deansgate area adding a contemporary flair to the cityscape. MediaCityUK in Salford, just outside the city center, is a good example of modern urban design, functioning as a hub for media and creative businesses while giving a range of recreational and culinary alternatives.

The revitalization of areas such as the Northern Quarter has transformed them into trendy districts known for their independent shops, street art, and eclectic eateries. These areas provide a stark contrast to the traditional industrial buildings, highlighting Manchester's ability to evolve and adapt while maintaining its unique character.

Learning and Creativity

Prestigious universities like Manchester Metropolitan University and the University of Manchester are located in Manchester, which is also a hub for innovation and education. These universities attract students and researchers from around the world, fostering a spirit of creativity and intellectual curiosity. Young professionals and creatives find Manchester to be an appealing destination because to the city's strong tech and startup culture, which is bolstered by programs that promote entrepreneurship and innovation.

Recreation and Green Areas

Despite its urban landscape, Manchester offers an abundance of green spots where tourists may relax and unwind. Heaton Park, one of the largest municipal parks in Europe, provides enormous places for picnicking, sports, and leisurely walks. Fletcher Moss Botanical Garden offers a tranquil environment with lovely vegetation and scenic walking routes. Additionally, the recently created parks and waterfront areas along the River Irwell and the Manchester Ship Canal provide magnificent locations for outdoor sports and gatherings.

Culinary Excellence

Manchester has a vast array of dining alternatives to suit every taste and budget, reflecting the diversity of its population. From traditional British pubs serving substantial meals to Michelin-starred restaurants offering gourmet experiences, the city caters to all gastronomic interests. The Northern Quarter is particularly famous for its independent cafes, artisan bakeries, and innovative restaurants, making it a hotspot for food enthusiasts. Furthermore, street food markets such as Arndale Market and Mackie Mayor offer a diverse range of international flavours, enabling tourists to experience multiple cuisines in one place.

Connectivity and Accessibility

Manchester is well-connected both domestically and internationally, making it an easily accessible destination for travelers. Manchester Airport is one of the busiest in the UK, carrying flights to various global locations. The city's comprehensive public transportation network, including buses, trams, and trains, guarantees that travelling around is convenient and efficient. Manchester Piccadilly Station acts as a significant train hub, giving direct links to other major cities such as London, Liverpool, and Edinburgh.

Manchester is a city of contrasts and harmony, where historic charm meets modern innovation, and cultural diversity creates a vibrant and inclusive environment. Whether you're exploring its rich industrial heritage, immersing yourself in its dynamic arts scene, or enjoying its diverse culinary offerings, Manchester promises a memorable and enriching experience. As you navigate this guide, let it be your essential companion, providing up-to-date information, beautiful photos, and detailed maps to help you make the most of your visit to this extraordinary city in 2024 and 2025. Greetings from Manchester, a city full of exciting adventures waiting to be discovered around every turn.

How to Use This Guide

Greetings from your perfect 2024 travel buddy to Manchester! Whether you are coming back to see more of this energetic city or are planning your first trip, this guide is meant to make the process easy and enjoyable. Here's how to make the most of the tools and information offered to ensure you experience Manchester to its maximum.

Getting About the Layout

This book has been carefully arranged into parts that are each focused on a distinct area of your trip and are easy to read and navigate. From lodging and food to entertainment and travel, every chapter offers in-depth information to make your planning easier. To locate the information you need quickly, refer to the table of contents at the beginning of the guide.

Making Use of the Maps

The thorough maps that are given in each section of this guide are one of its best qualities. By emphasising important sites, these maps make it simple to see how attractions, dining options, and lodging are arranged in relation to one another. Whether you choose to explore on foot, by automobile, or by public transportation, the maps will assist you in making an effective itinerary. Furthermore, our companion website offers interactive online maps with GPS capability for on-the-go navigation and real-time updates.

Investigating Current Data

Manchester is a city that is always changing, so you can be sure you have access to the most recent information with our guide. Every area is updated on a regular basis to take into account events, new openings, and modifications to local laws or transit schedules. If there are any last-minute alterations or noteworthy events taking place while you are here, make sure to check the "Latest Updates" area. This guarantees that your plans are accurate and up to date at all times.

Utilising the Images to Their Fullest
Since a picture speaks a thousand words, our guide makes use of exquisite photography to provide you with a visual overview of the experience. High-quality photos accompany each significant site and neighbourhood, allowing you to better understand the atmosphere and distinctive features of each place. Choose which places you are most eager to visit and use these pictures as inspiration for your itinerary.

Creating Your Schedule

Use the extensive lists offered to determine your top sights and must-do activities. Detailed descriptions and insider advice are available to help you prioritise your trips, regardless of your interests, be they history, the arts, sports, or fine dining. Take the suggested itineraries as a starting point and work your way down to suit your interests and the length of your visit. Remember to allow time for impromptu explorations—some of Manchester's most memorable moments can be discovered outside the usual route.

Lodging and Dining

Securing the ideal lodging and dining spots is essential for an unforgettable journey. Our lodging section offers a variety of choices, ranging from beautiful bed-and-breakfasts and opulent hotels to affordable hostels and serviced flats. Every listing has the pertinent information, including contact data, location, and facilities, as well as advice on which neighbourhoods might be best for you.

The dining area features a variety of dishes, including both international and traditional British fare, to highlight Manchester's vibrant culinary culture. Find renowned eateries, undiscovered treasures, and well-liked locations for street food. To help you fully enjoy the city's diverse flavours, each recommendation comes with a brief description, address, and any noteworthy specialities.

Navigating
To navigate Manchester easily, one must be aware of its transport system. In-depth details about buses, trams, and trains are available in our guide, along with advice on buying tickets and utilising travel passes. For individuals who would like to explore on their own, we also provide information on bike routes, taxi services, and rental cars.

Expert Advice and Regional Perspectives

Our guide has a plethora of insider knowledge and local insights to help you make the most of your trip. Find out when is the best time to visit well-known sites, where to get the finest city views, and how to get around the masses of tourists. Explore lesser-known attractions that are not usually included in tourist guides, and learn more about Manchester's distinctive customs and culture by reading our carefully chosen local tales and anecdotes.

Safety and Useful Information

Our first goals are your comfort and safety. To guarantee a worry-free journey, this book offers crucial details on regional regulations, emergency contacts, medical facilities, and safety advice. Learn the manners and customs of the area to improve your interactions with both locals and other tourists.

Using Extra Resources

For much more thorough information, visit our companion website, which features interactive maps, downloadable PDFs, and real-time updates. Stay up to date on events, travel advice, and news by following us on social media to make your trip to Manchester exciting and novel.

This comprehensive travel guide to Manchester is designed to be your go-to source for all the information you need to organise and have a great trip in 2024–2025. In one of the most vibrant cities in the UK, you may create a unique and memorable experience by utilising the current information, striking images, and thorough maps. Explore, dive in, and let this guide take you to all of Manchester's wonders. Greetings and best of luck on your travels!

Chapter 1: Getting to Manchester

Transportation Options

Making the most of your trip to this energetic city requires being able to navigate Manchester with ease. Manchester provides a wide variety of transportation options to meet the demands of every traveler, whether they choose the effectiveness of public transportation, the independence of cycling, or the convenience of taxis. Stunning images, current information, and thorough maps are all included in this section of your indispensable companion to help you navigate the city with ease in 2024 and 2025.

Transportation by Public

With Manchester's vast and dependable public transit system, exploring the entire city and its environs is a breeze.

Tram System Metrolink

The core of Manchester's public transport network is the Metrolink tram system, which provides wide coverage throughout the city and its suburbs. Metrolink connects important locations such the city centre, Manchester Airport, Salford Quays, and the University of Manchester with over 90 stops and various routes. Trams make frequent runs from early in the morning until late at night, so you can travel in comfort all day long. Tram stops, the Transport for Greater Manchester (TfGM) website, and the TfGM mobile app—which offers real-time service updates—are the three places where tickets can be bought.

Transportation Services

In addition to offering thorough coverage and reaching locations that Metrolink does not, buses are a valuable asset to the tram network. Many lines are operated by companies like as Stagecoach and First Manchester, which link residential areas, business centres, and tourist destinations. Buses are an affordable means of getting around the city; they run often and have long operating hours. For unrestricted travel, think about getting a day pass or a weekly travelcard. If you intend to ride the bus a lot while here, this can save you money.

Train Services

Another great choice for local and regional travel is Manchester's train system. The primary hub is Manchester Piccadilly Station, which provides direct links to important destinations like Edinburgh, London, Liverpool, and Leeds. Northern Rail offers regular intra-city services to several locations inside Manchester and its neighbouring towns. The journey is made comfortable and efficient by the recently renovated stations and contemporary trains. You can purchase single, return, or day tickets to fit your schedule online, at station kiosks, or through mobile apps.

Cycling

Cycling is a great way to see Manchester for people who lead active lives. The city has made large investments in the infrastructure needed for bicycling, creating safe and pleasurable routes with designated bike lanes.

Cycle Santander

Manchester's public bike-sharing program, Santander Cycles, provides a cost-effective and adaptable mode of transportation. You may rent a bike for short outings or longer excursions with ease because there are plenty of docking stations scattered around the city centre and important districts. Pay-as-you-go and annual pass membership options offer flexibility according to your travel schedule. You can easily manage your rentals, find nearby bikes, and check availability with the help of the user-friendly mobile app.

Tours and Bike Rentals

A variety of bike rental companies provide a wide selection of bicycles, from ordinary models to electric bikes and mountain bikes, if you would prefer a private cycling experience. There are also guided bike tours available, which let you see Manchester's top attractions through the eyes of an informed local guide. These trips offer a distinctive viewpoint on the city's rich past and dynamic present and frequently stop at parks, historic monuments, and cultural attractions.

Strolling

Manchester has a lot of attractions that are close to one another and is a very walkable city. Strolling around the city lets you experience its ambiance to the fullest, find hidden treasures, and take in the varied street art and architecture that embellish its neighbourhoods.

Walking Routes and Trails

Take a stroll around famous neighbourhoods including Castlefield, Deansgate, and the Northern Quarter to see the unique blend of new skyscrapers, old buildings, and lively street scenes. There are several walking paths and self-guided tours that offer insightful information about Manchester's history and culture while emphasising important areas of interest. You will find it easy to navigate the pedestrian-friendly streets of the city if you bring along comfortable shoes and this guide's map.

Ride-sharing and Taxis

In addition, Manchester has easy access to ride-sharing services such as Uber and taxis. You can use mobile apps, phone reservations, or street hailing to hail a taxi. For excursions to regions that are difficult to reach by public transportation or for late-night travel, ride-sharing provides a convenient and frequently affordable option.

Accredited Taxi Companies

A dependable choice that guarantees professionalism and safety are licensed black taxis. These cabs are available at specially designated taxi ranks, especially in the vicinity of the airport and Manchester Piccadilly Station, two important transportation hubs. Travellers can feel transparent and at ease knowing that prices are controlled.

Vehicle Rentals

Even though Manchester has an extensive public transport system, renting a car might provide you more freedom, particularly if you want to travel with family or friends or want to explore the surrounding areas. From Manchester Airport and the city centre, a plethora of car rental companies operate, providing a broad selection of automobiles to accommodate various needs and price ranges.

Parking and Road Safety Advice

Should you decide to drive, keep in mind that parking in the city centre might be costly and difficult. To locate open spots, look for park-and-ride choices or utilise parking applications. To guarantee a seamless and hassle-free journey, familiarise yourself with local driving laws, such as speed limits and parking regulations. For more effective street navigation in the city, think about hiring a car with a GPS system or utilising the navigation app on your smartphone.

Usability

Manchester is dedicated to providing accessibility for all guests. Accessible public transportation solutions for people with mobility impairments include priority seating on buses, low-floor trams and step-free access at stations. All of Manchester's amenities are accessible, as seen by the accessibility of many of the city's activities and lodging options.

Manchester's varied transit choices guarantee that every visitor can get around the city with ease and effectiveness. Whether you would rather go by public transportation, bike, stroll, or have the flexibility of a rental car, Manchester has everything you need to discover its bustling streets and undiscovered gems. Use this guide's comprehensive maps, current information, and useful advice to confidently plan your travels. Accept how simple it is to navigate Manchester and concentrate on making lifelong experiences in one of the most vibrant cities in the UK.

Navigating the City

Your trip will be enhanced if you can easily explore Manchester and immerse yourself in its dynamic culture, extensive history, and cutting-edge attractions. This portion of your indispensable travel companion offers thorough directions for getting around Manchester, so you can make the most of your trip between 2024 and 2025. With its breathtaking photographs, up-to-date information, and comprehensive maps, it has everything you need to navigate the city with ease and effectiveness.

Recognising Manchester's Architecture

Manchester is a large city with a variety of neighbourhoods, each with its own special charm and things to do. Being familiar with the layout of the city will make it easier for you to plan your trips. The city centre, which is home to important landmarks, retail areas, and cultural venues, is the centre of activity. From hip stores and street art to historical sites and waterfront promenades, the surrounding neighbourhoods of Salford, the Northern Quarter, and the Deansgate sector provide a variety of experiences.

Public Transport

Many visitors use Manchester's public transport system because it is dependable and comprehensive.

Tram System Metrolink

The core of Manchester's public transport system is the Metrolink tram system, which has over 90 stops spread over several routes. It links important locations like Salford's MediaCityUK, Manchester Airport, the city centre, and well-liked neighbourhoods like Deansgate and Piccadilly. Trams are a handy means of transportation across the city, operating often from early in the morning until midnight. Tram stops, the Transport for Greater Manchester (TfGM) website, and the TfGM mobile app—which provides real-time service updates—are the three locations where tickets can be bought.

Transportation Services

Manchester's bus services supplement the tram network by reaching regions not served by Metrolink. Companies such as Stagecoach and First Manchester provide a multitude of routes that link residential areas, business districts, and tourist destinations. Buses are an affordable choice that have long operation hours and frequent departures. Buying a day pass or weekly travelcard can provide unlimited travel and can be particularly cost-effective if you want to ride the bus frequently during your visit.

Train Services

Manchester's train network is a great option for longer trips or regional transport. The primary rail hub is Manchester Piccadilly Station, which offers direct trains to major cities like Edinburgh, London, Liverpool, and Leeds. Northern Rail provides regular services across the city to different areas of Manchester and neighbouring towns, so you can get where you are going with ease. Single, return, and day passes are available for purchase on the internet, at station kiosks, and through mobile apps, providing customers with flexibility.

Cycling in Manchester

Cycling is a popular and eco-friendly way to explore Manchester, supported by an expanding network of bike lanes and dedicated routes.

Cycle Santander

Manchester's public bike-sharing program, Santander Cycles, provides a cost-effective and adaptable choice for quick travels within the city. Renting a bike is easy and convenient because there are plenty of docking stations scattered around the city centre and important locations. You can find available bikes, monitor the status of docking stations, and manage your rentals while on the road using the easy-to-use smartphone app. Pay-as-you-go rates and annual passes are among the membership choices that accommodate various travel demands.

Tours and Bike Rentals

Several bike rental companies provide a variety of bicycles, including electric bikes and mountain bikes, for people who want a more customised cycling experience. Furthermore, guided bike tours offer an interesting approach to see Manchester's top attractions while learning from an experienced local guide. These excursions provide a greater insight of the city's history and current developments, and frequently include stops at parks, historic sites, and cultural monuments.

Manchester Walking

Manchester has a lot of attractions that are close to one another and is a very walkable city. Strolling around the city lets you take in its varied architecture, active street life, and hidden treasures.

Well-liked Walking Paths

Explore iconic places such as the Northern Quarter, famed for its unique mix of independent stores and street art, or wander along Canal Street in Castlefield, where old canals meet modern cafés and pubs. The Deansgate neighbourhood is ideal for an urban walking tour because it has a mix of modern skyscrapers and old buildings. There are themed trails and self-guided walking tours that highlight major attractions and offer insightful information about Manchester's past and present.

Ride-sharing and Taxis

In addition, Manchester has easy access to ride-sharing services such as Uber and taxis. Taxis are an adaptable and frequently affordable alternative to public transport, particularly for late-night travel or excursions to places that are difficult to reach by conventional means. They can be called, reserved on the spot, or accessed through smartphone apps.

Accredited Taxi Companies

A dependable choice that guarantees professionalism and safety are licensed black taxis. These cabs are available at specially designated taxi ranks, especially in the vicinity of the airport and Manchester Piccadilly Station, two important transportation hubs. Travellers can feel transparent and at ease knowing that prices are controlled.

Vehicle Rentals

Even though Manchester has an extensive public transport system, renting a car might provide you more freedom, particularly if you want to travel with family or friends or want to explore the surrounding areas. From Manchester Airport and the city centre, a plethora of car rental companies operate, providing a broad selection of automobiles to accommodate various needs and price ranges.

Parking and Road Safety Advice

Understanding Manchester traffic patterns and parking laws is necessary when driving there. Parking in the city centre can be difficult and pricey, so to find spots, think about using park-and-ride lots or parking applications. To guarantee a seamless and hassle-free journey, familiarise yourself with local driving laws, such as speed limits and parking restrictions. You can also get around the city's streets more quickly by using the navigation software on your smartphone or by hiring a car with a GPS system.

Usability

Manchester is dedicated to providing accessibility for all guests. Accessible public transportation solutions for people with mobility impairments include priority seating on buses, low-floor trams and step-free access at stations. Accessible lodgings and attractions abound in Manchester, making it possible for everyone to take advantage of everything the city has to offer.

Manchester's varied and well-connected transit options make getting around easy. Manchester gives you all the resources you need to easily explore its bustling streets and secret corners, whether your preference is for the effectiveness of public transit, the independence of cycling, the ease of walking, or the convenience of taxis and ride-sharing services. Use this guide's comprehensive maps, current information, and helpful advice to confidently plan your travels. Accept how simple it is to navigate Manchester and concentrate on making lifelong experiences in one of the most vibrant cities in the UK.

Chapter 2: Top Attractions

Manchester, a city full of innovation, culture, and history, has a wide range of top tourist destinations to suit all kinds of visitors. Manchester offers guests remarkable experiences in 2024 and beyond, with its famous buildings, top-notch museums, energetic neighbourhoods, and breathtaking green areas. To assist you in navigating and taking advantage of everything the city has to offer, this part highlights the must-see sites and is enhanced with current information, eye-catching pictures, and thorough maps.

Manchester Museum

An invaluable resource for natural history, archaeology, and anthropology, the Manchester

Museum is a mainstay of the city's cultural landscape. This museum, which is housed on the University of Manchester campus, has an amazing collection that includes dinosaur skeletons and artefacts from ancient Egypt. It is a favourite among history buffs and families alike because of its interactive exhibits and captivating displays. Do not miss the magnificent Victoria Gallery of Zoology, which features exquisitely arranged exhibitions of a wide variety of animal specimens.

The Lowry

The Lowry, a leading arts and entertainment centre named for the well-known artist L.S. Lowry, is located in the bustling Salford Quays. Two theatres in the complex present a range of performances, such as live music, dance, and drama. The Lowry also has a sizable collection of Lowry's well-known works, which, with their characteristic "matchstick men" figures, perfectly capture the spirit of Manchester's industrial heritage. The Salford Quays neighbourhood, with its stylish eateries, modern buildings, and waterfront vistas, is ideal for a leisurely stroll.

John Rylands Library

A must-see destination for fans of literature and history is the John Rylands Library. This neo-Gothic masterpiece, part of the University of Manchester, is home to an unparalleled collection of rare books and manuscripts, including a Gutenberg Bible and early works by William Shakespeare. The magnificent design of the library creates a calm and stimulating atmosphere for exploration with its elaborate masonry and regal reading rooms. More insights into the library's remarkable holdings and illustrious past are provided by guided tours.

Manchester Art Gallery

The Manchester Art Gallery is a must-see location for art lovers. This gallery, which is right in the middle of the city, has a large collection of British and European art, including both modern and classical treasures. Pieces by well-known artists including Turner, Hockney, and Bacon are among the highlights. Every visit to the gallery is different because of the special events, educational activities, and rotating exhibitions that it organises. The exquisitely designed gallery gardens provide an ideal area for unwinding and contemplating the artwork.

Trafford Old

A trip to Manchester would not be complete without seeing the storied Old Trafford, which is the home of the Manchester United Football Club. Often referred to as the "Theatre of Dreams," this legendary stadium is a global destination for football enthusiasts. Experience the rich history of the stadium on a guided tour, see the players' dressing rooms, and peruse the museum's remarkable trophy collection. Whether you are a devoted fan or just a casual spectator, match days offer an amazing atmosphere and an experience that you will not soon forget.

The Northern Quarter

Manchester's bohemian centre, the Northern Quarter, is well-known for its unique blend of independent stores, hip bars, and colourful street art. For those looking for a more alternative and artistic side of the city, this bustling neighbourhood is ideal. Explore unusual businesses selling vintage apparel, handmade jewelry, and eccentric homeware. With a variety of cafes, gastropubs, and international restaurants offering delectable and inventive cuisine, the region is also a mecca for foodies. The Sunday markets are a must-visit location for anything from fresh local vegetables to handcrafted goods.

Park Heaton

For a reprieve from the daily buzz, Heaton Park offers a huge green retreat just minutes from the city center. It is one of Europe's biggest municipal parks, with expansive woodlands, picturesque lakes, and exquisitely designed gardens that are ideal for strolling, cycling, and picnics. All year long, the park also holds a variety of events and activities, such as outdoor concerts, fairs, and sporting competitions. The gorgeous neo-classical palace Heaton Hall and the quaint miniature train, which is a family and kid favourite, are two of Heaton Park's main attractions.

Museum of Science and Industry

Celebrating Manchester's key role in the Industrial Revolution, the Science and Industry Museum is a fascinating destination for visitors of all ages. Located on the site of the world's first passenger railway station, the museum provides interactive displays that dive into the city's technological advances and industrial past. Highlights include the original textile factory machinery, the antique steam engines, and interesting exhibits about contemporary scientific and technological advancements. Learning is entertaining and educational thanks to the museum's engaging programs and practical activities.

Manchester Cathedral

Encrusted with historical significance, Manchester Cathedral is a magnificent illustration of Gothic design and a tranquil haven amidst the busy metropolis. Dating back to the 15th century, the cathedral has exquisite stained glass windows, elaborate stone sculptures, and a quiet cloister garden. The magnificent chapter house, the serene Chapter House Library, and the breathtaking nave are open for exploration by guests. In addition, the cathedral regularly sponsors community gatherings, art exhibits, and concerts, serving as the city's spiritual and cultural hub.

Campus Etihad

The Etihad Campus is a contemporary marvel for fans of sports and architecture. This cutting-edge facility, which houses the Manchester City Football Club, has the magnificent Etihad

Stadium, training grounds, and the City Football Academy. The City Football Academy Museum, which is located on the site, provides information to supporters about the history, accomplishments, and goals of the team. Beautifully built public spaces surround the campus, making it a fun place to visit before or after a game.

The best places to visit in Manchester provide a varied and enriching experience that reflects the city's distinctive fusion of modernity, culture, and history. There is something for everyone to enjoy, whether you choose to explore the past at the John Rylands Library, take in world-class art at the Manchester Art Gallery, or simply take in the lively atmosphere of the Northern Quarter. Utilise the most recent information, gorgeous images, and thorough maps provided in this book to explore and take advantage of everything Manchester has to offer. While visiting Manchester in 2024 and 2025, embrace the energy of this vibrant city and make lifelong memories.

Historical Sites

Manchester, a city linked to modern innovation and the Industrial Revolution, is full with historical sites that provide insight into its revolutionary past. Manchester's historical sites, which range from magnificent Victorian architecture to preserved industrial landmarks, are essential to comprehending the development and cultural legacy of the city. This portion of your indispensable travel companion focusses on the historical landmarks that you simply must see. It is enhanced with current information, eye-catching images, and thorough maps to make your exploration of Manchester in 2024 and beyond even more enjoyable.

Town Hall in Manchester

Manchester Town Hall is a stunning example of Victorian Gothic Revival architecture, standing tall and proud in the centre of the city. The renowned architect Alfred Waterhouse created this magnificent structure, which was finished in 1877 and today houses the Manchester City Council. The striking façade of the Town Hall, with its elaborate stone carvings and tall spires, is evidence of the wealth of the city throughout the Industrial Revolution. Inside, guests may take in the magnificent Marble Hall, the stately council chambers, and a variety of artwork displays that pay homage to Manchester's rich cultural past. There are available guided tours that provide information on the architectural significance and history of the structure.

John Rylands Library

One of Manchester's most prized historical buildings is the John Rylands Library, a refuge for book lovers and history buffs. Part of the University of Manchester, this neo-Gothic library was founded in 1900 and holds an extensive collection of rare books, manuscripts, and archives. A Gutenberg Bible, illuminated manuscripts from the Middle Ages, and original writings by literary greats like William Shakespeare are among its treasured possessions. The magnificent design of the library exudes timeless elegance with its elaborate masonry and lofty ceilings. Visitors can explore the reading rooms, galleries, and wonderfully planted gardens, making it a great blend of history and peace.

Manchester Cathedral

With roots in the fifteenth century, Manchester Cathedral, often referred to as the Cathedral and Collegiate Church of St. Mary, is a remarkable example of Gothic architecture. Located near the River Irwell, the cathedral has been a spiritual and architectural symbol for centuries. Its magnificent nave, elaborate stained glass windows, and elaborate chapels provide a calm haven from the busy metropolis. The cathedral has hosted key civic and religious events, and it has a considerable historical significance as well. Take a guided tour to discover more about the building's historical significance, architectural elements, and the lives of the worshippers who have come before them.

The Whitworth

The Whitworth, which was first built as a textile mill in the middle of the 19th century, has been completely renovated into a top-notch art gallery that skilfully combines old and new architecture. The University of Manchester's gallery, located in Whitworth Park, features an outstanding collection of fine art, textiles, and contemporary installations. The building itself is an intriguing blend of contemporary additions and historic industrial buildings that captures Manchester's transition from an industrial powerhouse to a hub for the arts and culture. For anyone interested in the interaction between history and modernity, the Whitworth's inventive exhibitions and stunning park location make it a must-visit.

Castlefield

Manchester's historic centre, Castlefield, provides a unique window into the city's industrial past. Once the hub of Manchester's canal system, this neighbourhood is today a bustling community that embraces contemporary advancements while retaining its historic charm. Explore the Bridgewater Canal, the intact canal locks, and the abandoned warehouses and mills that have been converted into hip pubs, eateries, and cultural centres. The famous Cobden Bridge, the Museum of Science and Industry, and the Roman fort at Castlefield are among the attractions. Castlefield offers a vibrant setting for both leisurely strolls and in-depth historical investigation thanks to its seamless integration of history and modern life.

The Library of Chetham

Founded in 1653, Chetham's Library is the oldest public library in the English-speaking world. The library, housed within Chetham's School of Music, is home to a vast collection of antiquarian books, manuscripts, and printed works spanning several centuries. The library's ancient reading rooms provide a calm, academic setting with their oak panelling and antique furnishings. The outstanding collection, which features early printings of literary masterpieces and significant historical records, is on display for visitors to peruse. In addition to being a storehouse of knowledge, Chetham's Library is a masterfully maintained historical monument that embodies Manchester's enduring dedication to culture and education.

Ancoats

Ancoats, which was formerly the centre of Manchester's textile industry, is experiencing a revival while maintaining its historic industrial legacy. Some of the oldest mills and warehouses still standing in the city may be found in this historic region; many of them have been transformed into contemporary lofts, cafes, and creative spaces. While strolling through Ancoats, one may observe the architectural elements and brickwork that are reminiscent of the area's industrial heritage. The Marble Arch, a magnificent example of Italianate architecture, and the Manchester Grain Exchange are two important attractions. Ancoats is an interesting neighbourhood to explore because of its unique mix of old and new, providing insights into Manchester's transformation from an industrial hub to a bustling, modern neighbourhood.

The historical sites of Manchester provide an engrossing trip down memory lane, illustrating the city's incredible metamorphosis from an industrial giant to a cutting-edge cultural hub. Every location offers a different perspective on the rich history of the city, whether you are admiring the architectural magnificence of Manchester Town Hall, exploring the rare collections of the John Rylands Library, or meandering along the picturesque canals of Castlefield. Make the most of this guide's up-to-date information, gorgeous images, and thorough maps to explore and fully appreciate Manchester's historical treasures. Accept the legends and sites that define

Manchester's history and allow them to enhance your trip through one of the most vibrant cities in the UK.

Museums and Galleries

Manchester, a city known for its thriving cultural scene and rich industrial background, is home to an amazing selection of museums and galleries that appeal to a wide range of interests. Manchester's museums and galleries have something to offer everyone, regardless of your interests—you can be an art aficionado, a history buff, or just inquisitive about the vibrant culture of the city. The best museums and galleries are highlighted in this area of your indispensable guide, together with the most recent information, eye-catching images, and thorough maps to enable you to explore and properly appreciate Manchester's artistic and historical treasures in 2024 and beyond.

Manchester Museum

A vital component of the city's cultural landscape, the Manchester Museum is situated on the University of Manchester campus. It was founded in 1867 and has a vast collection including anthropology, archaeology, and natural history. Visitors can marvel at anything from ancient Egyptian treasures to Roman antiques to a thorough display of dinosaur skeletons. The museum is a favourite with history aficionados and families alike because of its captivating displays and interactive exhibits. Immersion into the natural world is provided by the magnificent collection of animal species on display in the recently refurbished Victoria Gallery of Zoology. Programs for education and touring exhibitions guarantee that there is always something fresh to learn.

The Whitworth

Situated within Whitworth Park, The Whitworth is Manchester's flagship art gallery, beautifully integrating historical building with contemporary design. The gallery was once built as a textile mill in the middle of the 19th century and has since been renovated to become a premier location that honours fine art and textiles. Whitworth's remarkable collection consists of current artworks that challenge the conventions of modern art as well as pieces by well-known painters including Turner, Hockney, and Bacon. Every visit to the gallery is different because it regularly organises events, seminars, and temporary exhibitions. Visitors can enjoy art and nature in one visit by strolling through the neighbouring park, which offers a gorgeous environment.

Manchester Art Gallery

Art enthusiasts should not miss the Manchester Art Gallery, which is situated right in the middle of the city. The gallery has a collection of about 25,000 pieces of European and British art that spans seven centuries. Pre-Raphaelite masterworks, breathtaking Impressionist paintings, and modern installations are among the highlights. The gallery is particularly noted for its amazing collection of decorative arts, including pottery, textiles, and metalwork. There is always something new to discover thanks to interactive exhibits and exhibitions that change frequently. The exquisitely designed gallery gardens offer a calm setting in which to unwind and consider the artwork.

The Lowry

The Lowry, a leading arts and entertainment centre named for the well-known artist L.S. Lowry, is situated in the bustling Salford Quays. Two theatres in the complex present a range of performances, such as live music, dance, and drama. The Lowry is also home to a sizable collection of Lowry's well-known works, which, with their characteristic "matchstick men" figures, perfectly capture the spirit of Manchester's industrial heritage. The Salford Quays neighbourhood, with its stylish eateries, modern buildings, and waterfront vistas, is ideal for a leisurely stroll. The Lowry is a vibrant cultural centre that draws tourists from all over thanks to its interactive exhibitions and events.

Museum of Science and Industry

The Science and Industry Museum, which honours Manchester's crucial role in the Industrial Revolution, is an engaging experience for guests of all ages. Situated on the location of the initial passenger train station globally, the museum presents interactive displays that explore the technological innovations and industrial legacy of the city. Historic steam engines, authentic textile factory machinery, and interesting exhibits on cutting-edge scientific and technological advancements are among the attractions' highlights. Learning is entertaining and educational thanks to the museum's engaging programs and practical activities. There is always something new to discover thanks to special exhibitions and events, which combine education and enjoyment in the ideal amount.

North of the Imperial War Museum

Daniel Libeskind created the stunning Imperial War Museum North, an immersive and impactful architectural monument. The museum, which is situated near Salford Quays, investigates how contemporary conflicts affect individuals and society. Its distinctive, angular shape represents a globe torn apart by battle, echoing the museum's emphasis on international conflict and its aftereffects. Visitors gain a profound awareness of the human cost of conflict through interactive displays, multimedia presentations, and thought-provoking installations. The museum is an essential component of Manchester's cultural landscape because it also holds talks, educational activities, and temporary exhibitions.

HOUSE Manchester

Manchester's premier venue for modern theatre, film, and art, HOME offers a dynamic environment for ingenuity and originality. Home is a varied program featuring indie films, provocative performances, and state-of-the-art art exhibitions. It is housed in the renovated Corn Exchange building. Globally renowned contemporary artists are exhibited in the gallery spaces, while a variety of mainstream and experimental plays are performed in the theatres. A vital hub of Manchester's creative sector, HOME encourages artistic expression and cross-cultural interaction. In addition, the location has a bar and café, making it the ideal place to unwind and talk about the events of the day.

Science and Industry Museum

The Museum of Science and Industry, which honours Manchester's crucial role in the Industrial Revolution, is an engaging attraction for tourists of all ages. Situated on the location of the initial passenger train station globally, the museum presents interactive displays that explore the technological innovations and industrial legacy of the city. Highlights include the original textile factory machinery, the antique steam engines, and interesting displays on contemporary scientific and technological advancements. Learning is entertaining and educational thanks to the museum's engaging programs and practical activities.

Manchester's galleries and museums provide a wide range of experiences that capture the distinct fusion of history, culture, and creativity of the city. There are a plethora of cultural gems to be found, whether you are looking through antiquated artefacts at the Manchester Museum, appreciating modern art at The Whitworth, or taking in the dramatic shows at The Lowry. Utilize the up-to-date information, breathtaking images, and precise maps in this book to navigate and fully appreciate the best that Manchester's museums and galleries have to offer. Discover one of the most dynamic and culturally diverse cities in the UK as you immerse yourself in its bustling cultural scene and make lifelong memories.

Parks and Outdoor Spaces

Manchester is well-known for its thriving metropolitan culture and rich industrial legacy. It also has an amazing selection of parks and outdoor areas that provide both locals and tourists with a welcome diversion from the bustle of the city. Manchester's parks offer a variety of settings for play, relaxation, and exploration, from large green spaces ideal for strolls to well-kept botanical gardens and vibrant recreation areas. The must-see parks and outdoor areas are highlighted in this section of your indispensable companion, which is enhanced with current data, gorgeous images, and thorough maps to help you take full advantage of Manchester's natural beauty in 2024 and beyond.

Park Heaton

With more than 600 acres of gorgeous scenery, Heaton Park is a genuine gem of Manchester and one of the biggest municipal parks in all of Europe. This large green area, which is only a few miles from the city centre, has something to offer everyone. Wander through the lovely forests, take leisurely strolls around the picturesque lakes, or stand at different locations to take in the breathtaking views. In addition, Heaton Park is home to the beautiful neo-classical palace known as Heaton Hall, which is encircled by lovely paths and formal gardens. The park has several recreational facilities, including golf courses, tennis courts, and a miniature railway, making it a wonderful destination for families and outdoor enthusiasts. There is always something exciting going on at Heaton Park because it offers a variety of events all year long, including sporting tournaments, outdoor concerts, and fairs.

The Botanical Garden at Fletcher Moss

Tucked away in the verdant suburb of Didsbury, the Fletcher Moss Botanical Garden is a tranquil haven showcasing an exquisite array of global flora. The 35 acres of this exquisitely landscaped park are organised into numerous thematic zones, such as the Tropical House, Woodland Walk, and Rock park. Discover unusual plant species, meander through colourful flower beds, and unwind beside peaceful ponds are all available to visitors. In addition, the garden has lovely

Victorian glasshouses that make it the ideal place for plant lovers and anyone looking for a tranquil getaway. Fletcher Moss Botanical Garden is a lovely destination for both casual tourists and devoted gardeners, thanks to its seasonal displays and educational events.

Whitworth Park

Whitworth Park, which is next to The Whitworth Art Gallery, is a tasteful fusion of modern architecture and natural elements that provides the ideal backdrop for the cultural events held there. Large lawns, exquisitely designed gardens, and a variety of trees that offer shade and tranquilly may all be found in the park. It is a great place to have picnics, take leisurely walks, or just relax after viewing the local art exhibits. Whitworth Park also holds several outdoor events, including art installations, live concerts, and community gatherings, making it a dynamic focus of activity. The park's attraction as a central green space in the city is enhanced by its close proximity to the University of Manchester, which contributes a youthful and energetic vitality.

Park at Platt Fields

Situated in Manchester's southern region, Platt Fields Park is an adaptable open area that accommodates an array of pursuits. The park is well-liked by families, sportsmen, and nature enthusiasts because of its lovely lakes, vast sports facilities, and well-kept playgrounds. Aside from playing soccer, cricket, and other outdoor games on the park's many sports fields, visitors can enjoy water-based activities like boating and fishing. Beautiful walking pathways, picnic spaces, and a wide range of plants and animals can all be found in Platt Fields Park, offering plenty of chances for leisure and enjoyment. Seasonal activities, such as outdoor festivals and flower exhibitions, enhance the park's lively ambiance all year round.

Water Park Chorlton

With its placid lakes and abundant vegetation, Chorlton Water Park provides a tranquil haven for anyone looking for a more private and quiet outdoor experience. The park, which is ideal for leisurely hikes, bird watching, and taking in the natural surroundings, is situated in the hip

Chorlton area. The vast spaces and well-kept paths make for a great environment for outdoor sports like cycling and jogging. In addition, a variety of species can be found at Chorlton Water Park, which makes it a fun place for nature lovers to view the local flora and fauna. The park's calm environment and stunning splendour make it a perfect destination for visitors wishing to unwind and connect with nature.

Rochdale Canal

One of Manchester's oldest canals, the Rochdale Canal, provides a singular outdoor experience that blends cultural legacy and scenic beauty. Walking, cycling, and boating are all excellent activities along the canal, which stretches for kilometres through scenic rural and urban settings. Enjoying the peace and quiet of the waterway, tourists can take in picturesque views, quaint locks, and ancient bridges while strolling along the canal's towpath. There are lots of parks and green areas along the Rochdale Canal, making picnics and outdoor activities very possible. If you are looking for an exciting boat trip or a calm stroll, the Rochdale Canal is a must-see outdoor location in Manchester.

Sackville Park

Located in the Rusholme district, Sackville Park is a well-liked public area that provides a blend of leisure amenities and scenic views. Large, lush lawns, old trees, and a range of sporting facilities, such as tennis courts and a bowling green, may all be found in the park. The park has a well-equipped playground that is sure to please families, as well as running routes and outdoor workout equipment for fitness aficionados. In addition, Sackville Park holds seasonal fairs, outdoor concerts, and community events that engage people of all ages and promote a strong feeling of community.

Visitors can effortlessly blend an exciting outdoor day with the lively local culture thanks to its handy position close to the busy Chorlton Street.

Manchester's parks and outdoor areas offer a peaceful haven, leisure activities, and unspoiled beauty for everyone to enjoy, making them the ideal counterpoint to the city's urban setting. Manchester's many parks accommodate every taste and interest, whether you are looking for a serene garden stroll, an exciting sports day, or a picturesque place to stop and decompress. Make the most of this guide's current information, gorgeous pictures, and thorough maps to discover and enjoy all that Manchester has to offer when it comes to outdoor activities. Enjoy the green areas of the city and make lifelong memories amid the luscious scenery and energetic neighbourhoods that characterise Manchester's rustic appeal.

Chapter 3: Culinary Experiences

Must-Try Dishes

Manchester's diverse population, inventive attitude, and strong industrial background all contribute to the city's dynamic food culture. Manchester provides a great selection of must-try delicacies that reflect its dynamic culture, catering to both international and local palates. This portion of your indispensable travel companion showcases the best dining experiences, enhanced with current data, scrumptious images, and comprehensive maps to help you navigate the city's culinary scene in 2024 and beyond.

Customary British Cuisine

A trip to Manchester would not be complete without sampling some time-tested classic British cuisine.

Hotpot in Lancashire

Lancashire Hotpot is a mainstay of Manchester's traditional pubs, a hearty and comforting dish. Tender lamb or mutton is roasted to perfection after being piled with onions and diced potatoes in this slow-cooked stew. A hearty, flavourful dinner that warms you from the inside out is the end result. Savour this meal in landmark restaurants like as The Briton at Five Ways, where the real recipes and warm atmosphere make for a memorable dining experience.

Bury Pudding in Black

Black pudding is a savoury sausage made from swine fat, blood and oats that originated in nearby

Bury. It is a favourite addition to a classic English breakfast, but it is also good on its own or in other recipes. Visit eateries like Albert's Schloss to enjoy this treat along with creative takes on traditional cuisine and locally sourced ingredients.

Wide Range of Foreign Cuisines

Manchester is a sanctuary for foodies searching for flavours from around the world because to its diverse population, which has given rise to an eclectic mix of different cuisines.

Rusholme's Indian Curries

The Rusholme neighbourhood of Manchester is referred to as "Curry Mile" because of the wide variety of South Asian eateries it offers. The Curry Mile offers a wide variety of authentic Indian, Pakistani, and Bangladeshi curries to suit every taste, from creamy kormas to scorching vindaloos. Popular locations include Moti Mahal, which is well-known for its rich and fragrant meals that encapsulate Indian culinary traditions, and Bundobust, which serves traditional Indian street cuisine along with a selection of craft beers.

Mediterranean Meszze

Manchester is home to a plethora of Middle Eastern eateries that serve up mouthwatering falafel, hummus, shawarma, and mezze platters.

The city's mainstay, Aladdin's, is well-known for its flavourful dishes and fresh ingredients. Savour a leisurely lunch and a variety of small plates that highlight the region's vivid and varied flavours with your companions.

Fusion and Modern British Cooking

Manchester is home to a thriving modern British and fusion food scene that combines traditional ingredients with cutting-edge preparation methods.

Modern British Dishes at Australasia

With its modern British menu, Australasia, located in the fashionable Northern Quarter, provides a sophisticated dining experience. Traditional British gastronomy is reinvented with a modern touch in signature dishes like slow-cooked pork belly with seasonal vegetables and inventive desserts like sticky toffee pudding. For those interested in experiencing Manchester's culinary culture at the cutting edge, this place is a must-visit due to its chic setting and creative menu.

Dishoom's Fusion Flavours

Dishoom, a Manchester-based restaurant, combines Indian and British cuisine, drawing inspiration from the Irani cafés of Mumbai. Their menu offers a variety of dishes that combine ingredients and spices from both cultures to create flavours that are distinct and memorable. Do not miss their delicious house black daal, which strikes the ideal mix between tradition and innovation, or their famous bacon naan bread for breakfast.

Desserts and Sweet Treats

Manchester has an equally amazing dessert culture, with everything from classic candies to modern pleasures.

Eccles Cakes

Eccles Cakes, flaky pastries stuffed with currants and tinged with orange, are a must-try local treat. These delicious delicacies, named after the Greater Manchester town of Eccles, are available at bakeries all around the city. Visit the well-known Mackie Mayor market, where a number of sellers sell mouthwatering pastries in addition to freshly baked Eccles Cakes.

Cake Victoria Sponge

Popular in Manchester's cafes and patisseries, Victoria Sponge Cake is a classic British dessert. Usually filled with whipped cream and jam, this airy and light cake offers the ideal harmony of sweetness and structure. Enjoy a slice at the famed Koffee Pot Café, where the classic recipe is done to perfection, delivering a wonderful finale to any meal.

Markets and Street Cuisine

Manchester's lively markets and street food scene have plenty of tasty options to try for a more laid-back dining experience.

Arndale Market

Arndale Market, a vibrant centre of activity in the city, offers a diverse array of street food options from around the globe. With a wide variety of options available, the market guarantees that there is something to satisfy every taste, ranging from gourmet burgers and artisanal pizzas to exotic Asian and Middle Eastern cuisine. It is a well-liked location for both locals and tourists because of the vibrant atmosphere and reasonable costs.

Mayor Mackie

A wonderfully restored market building turned food hall, Mackie Mayor is located in the historic Cheetham Hill neighbourhood. You can browse a variety of street food vendors selling sushi, tacos, vegan snacks, and freshly baked goodies here. A leisurely meal with friends or family is the ideal environment thanks to the chic décor and common seating areas.

Manchester offers a wide variety of must-try foods to suit every taste and inclination, making its culinary scene as lively and varied as the city itself. Manchester offers a unique eating experience whether you are indulging in modern fusion dishes, sampling exotic cuisines, savouring classic British meals, or indulging in sweet pleasures. With the help of this guide's delicious images, comprehensive maps, and current information, you can easily explore the city's thriving food scene. In 2024 and 2025, while you explore this amazing city, embrace the tastes and culinary advancements that make Manchester a veritable food lover's dream and develop gastronomic experiences that will last a lifetime.

Popular Restaurants and Cafés

Manchester has a wide variety of well-liked eateries and cafés that satisfy every taste and inclination, making its culinary scene as vibrant and varied as the city itself. Manchester has a wide variety of dining options to suit all tastes, including fine dining, genuine international cuisine, and comfortable places to enjoy a leisurely cup of coffee. With the help of current data, captivating images, and thorough maps, this section of your indispensable companion showcases some of the most well-liked restaurants in the city, enabling you to explore and take advantage of everything Manchester has to offer in 2024 and beyond.

Australasia

Australasia, located in the hip Northern Quarter, is a noteworthy spot for modern British food with a contemporary touch. This restaurant offers a distinctive dining experience, blending Australian and Southeast Asian influences with style and innovation in its menu and interior design. Among the restaurant's signature dishes are the succulent lamb shoulder seasoned with Thai flavours and the delicious seafood platter made with fresh, regional ingredients. Australasia's lively ambience, along with its vast drink menu and remarkable wine selection, makes it an ideal location for both informal lunches and memorable feasts. It is best to reserve a table in advance because this well-liked location frequently fills up fast.

Dishoom Manchester

In the centre of the city, Dishoom Manchester offers a flavour of India, influenced by the Irani cafés of Mumbai. Situated in the historic Chorlton district, Dishoom is well-known for its genuine tastes, cosy atmosphere, and top-notch service. From the well-liked bacon naan roll for breakfast to the thick and flavourful house black daal, the menu offers a wide variety of options. Their freshly made bread and unique cocktails go very well with the colourful and fragrant food. Do not miss them. Dishoom's exquisitely furnished interiors, complete with antique pictures and artwork, provide a warm and welcoming ambiance that makes it a must-visit location for both residents and visitors.

Rudy's Pizza Neapolitana

Rudy's Neapolitan Pizza is a must-visit location for pizza enthusiasts. Rudy's, a popular pizza place in the Spinningfields neighbourhood, is well-known for its real Neapolitan pizzas that are baked to perfection in a wood-fired oven. The menu is simple but elegant, with traditional dishes like the Margherita, which has fresh mozzarella, basil, and tomato, and the Diavola, which has bold flavours and spicy salami. The open kitchen, where you can watch the pizzas being made, and the laid-back, energetic ambiance enhance the whole dining experience. Rudy's is a terrific place for a casual supper with friends or family because it also has a nice assortment of artisan beers and wines.

Albert's Schloss

Located in the centre of the Northern Quarter, Albert's Schloss is a popular restaurant and pub that serves a varied food in a boisterous ambiance. A distinctive and unforgettable eating experience can be had at Albert's Schloss, which is well-known for its quirky décor, which features neon lights, chandeliers, and vintage furniture. Highlights of the cuisine include the flavourful schnitzel and the sizzling bratwurst plate, which combine German and cosmopolitan influences. It is a well-liked location for both dinner and nightlife because of its comprehensive beverages menu, which offers a wide variety of beers, cocktails, and spirits. There is always something going on at Albert's Schloss thanks to live music performances and special nights.

Federal Café Bar

Nestled in the heart of Ancoats, Federal Café Bar is a local favourite, well-known for its delicious breakfast and brunch options. Federal, a popular Australian-style café, offers a delicious selection of dishes cooked using ingredients that are acquired locally and freshly. The rich avocado toast, the fluffy ricotta hotcakes, and the decadent bacon and egg roll are among the speciality dishes. The café's warm atmosphere is ideal for beginning the day thanks to its simple yet cosy design and helpful staff. In addition, Federal has a variety of speciality coffees, teas and fresh juices, which makes it the perfect place for a laid-back morning or a light conversation with friends.

Volta's The Refuge
The Refuge by Volta is a gastronomic paradise that blends gorgeous architecture with a creative and varied menu. It is located in the famous Principal Hotel on Deansgate. The room, which was created by famous architect Damien Hirst, has dramatic interiors with tall ceilings, elaborate decorations, and tasteful furniture. A blend of international cuisines can be found on The Refuge's menu, which has delicacies like truffle risotto, slow-cooked meats that are tender, and roasted cauliflower steak. A carefully chosen wine list, a variety of premium spirits, and inventive cocktails are all part of the vast beverages menu. The Refuge's elegant atmosphere makes it a great option for a special occasion, a memorable supper, or a chic night out.

Gil & Ezra

Ezra & Gil is a great option for those looking for a real Middle Eastern meal in the Northern Quarter. Traditional Lebanese and Mediterranean cuisine, served in flavourful, substantial amounts, is the restaurant's speciality. It is lively and colourful. Savoury shawarma platters, fragrant falafel, and flavourful hummus variants are among the favourites. A wonderful eating experience is ensured by the professional service and cosy, welcoming setting. In addition, Ezra & Gil has a wide range of vegan and vegetarian options, making it a flexible place for all dietary needs. In the centre of Manchester, Ezra & Gil offers a genuine experience of the Middle East, perfect for a leisurely lunch or a filling dinner.

Rudy's Café Bar

In the Northern Quarter, Rudy's Café Bar is a well-liked destination for people seeking a casual dinner in a welcoming atmosphere. Rudy's is well-known for its wide brunch menu, which includes creative avocado toasts, substantial breakfast bowls, and traditional eggs benedict. The café is well-liked by both locals and tourists due to its relaxed atmosphere, lovely décor, and welcoming staff. In the evening, Rudy's changes into a welcoming bar with a menu of delectable pub grub and a variety of craft beers, wines and cocktails. Rudy's Café Bar is a must-visit location in Manchester because of its delicious food, fantastic drinks, and cosy environment.

Popular eateries and cafés in Manchester provide a varied and fascinating culinary experience, showcasing the city's inventive energy and rich cultural tapestry. Every palate can be satisfied by the variety of options available, which range from classic British food and genuine world cuisines to contemporary fusion dishes and welcoming cafés. Make use of this guide's current information, alluring pictures, and thorough maps to discover and enjoy Manchester's greatest dining options. Indulging in a fine dining experience, taking pleasure in a laid-back brunch, or sipping a masterfully mixed cocktail—Manchester's lively eateries and cafés promise exceptional culinary experiences that will elevate your trip to this exciting city in 2024 and beyond.

Food Markets and Street Food

Manchester's gastronomic landscape is as rich in restaurants and cafés as it is in energetic food markets and lively street food vendors. These vibrant spaces provide a diverse range of tastes, cultures, and experiences, making them must-visits for any traveler who enjoys cuisine. Whether you're seeking gourmet delicacies, international cuisines, or distinctive local treats, Manchester's food markets and street food centres give an amazing gastronomic trip. The best food markets and street food spots are highlighted in this area of your indispensable companion, which is enhanced with current data, mouthwatering images, and thorough maps to help you explore and enjoy everything Manchester has to offer in 2024 and beyond.

Arndale Market

One of the UK's oldest and most famous food markets, Arndale Market is located right in the middle of Manchester's city centre. The market is a lively gathering place where locals and tourists come together to enjoy a wide variety of fresh vegetables, exotic specialities, and delicious street food. It is located several levels below the busy Arndale Shopping Centre. From fresh fruits and vegetables to artisanal cheeses and baked delicacies, Arndale Market offers a comprehensive assortment of high-quality items. A wide range of street food vendors providing everything from unique international dishes to classic British fare can be found in the food court area. Arndale Market provides something to sate every craving, whether it be for a thick pie, delectable kebabs, or cool smoothies.

Mayor Mackie

Located in the historic Cheetham Hill district, Mackie Mayor is a beautifully renovated Victorian market structure that has been turned into a vibrant food hall. A carefully chosen array of individual food sellers, each with their own distinctive culinary inventions, can be found at this hip location. A variety of cuisines are available for visitors to sample, such as sushi, vegan treats, artisanal pizzas, and gourmet burgers. Mackie Mayor is a great place for a casual dinner with friends or family because it has chic communal dining areas as well. The market's lively ambiance and lovely architecture make it the ideal place to sample a variety of cuisines and learn about Manchester's vibrant culinary scene. There is constantly something new to discover at Mackie Mayor because to regular events and themed culinary festivals, which offer an added element of excitement.

Food Markets in the Northern Quarter

There are many food markets and street food vendors in the Northern Quarter, which is well-known for its varied and artistic atmosphere, which capture the bohemian ethos of the neighbourhood. Every year, The Manchester Food and Drink Festival turns the Northern Quarter into a hive of food activity, complete with pop-up restaurants, gourmet food stalls, and street food vendors. The festival highlights the finest of Manchester's street food innovation, with everything from gourmet tacos and fusion burgers to artisanal sweets and speciality beverages. Smaller markets and pop-up gatherings showcase the Northern Quarter's varied culinary culture all year long, giving guests the chance to try out unusual and creative cuisine in a vibrant and creative setting.

Curry Mile

Manchester's famous Curry Mile in Rusholme is a must-visit location for food aficionados seeking real South Asian cuisine. This lively neighbourhood stretches along Wilmslow Road and is lined with a multitude of eateries, takeaways, and food booths serving a wide range of Middle Eastern, Indian, and Pakistani cuisine. For those who enjoy strong, aromatic flavours, the Curry Mile is a haven of flavour, offering everything from tasty naan breads to juicy kebabs and spicy curries and biryanis. For a filling supper on the run, quick and delectable options are offered by street food sellers and tiny restaurants. The vibrant ambiance and alluring smells emanating from the several restaurants make the Curry Mile a must-visit destination for foodies in Manchester.

Events and Festivals of Street Food

Manchester celebrates its rich culinary history all year long with a number of street food festivals and events. Manchester Street Food Festival: a carefully chosen collection of street food vendors providing a variety of creative dishes and international cuisines come together at various sites throughout the city. These festivals offer a great chance to try a variety of flavours, from classic street food favourites to innovative culinary concoctions. For foodies interested in discovering Manchester's exciting street food culture, these events are ideal because they include live music, entertainment, and vibrant atmospheres that improve the overall experience.

Advice for Savouring Street Food and Food Markets in Manchester

- Organise Your Visit: To make the most of your trip, check the food markets' and street food festivals' event calendars and working hours. Certain vendors may only be available on certain days or at certain times in certain markets.

- Carry Cash: Although a lot of merchants take credit cards, it is always a good idea to have extra cash on hand, especially for pop-up events or smaller stalls.

- Depart Early: You can avoid crowds and get the best food selection by getting there early. It's also a fantastic opportunity to explore the market before it becomes too hectic.

- Make a Novel Attempt: Do not be afraid to explore new foods and venture beyond your comfort zone. Manchester's varied food markets present a singular chance to sample a broad range of international cuisines.

Keep Yourself Hydrated: It is possible to walk a lot when exploring food markets, so be sure to stay hydrated by consuming lots of water or cool drinks from the vendors.

Manchester's food markets and street food scene are fundamental to the city's dynamic cultural fabric, delivering a wide and thrilling assortment of gastronomic experiences. There is no shortage of locations to explore and flavours to savour, from the bustling Curry Mile and the artistic

Northern Quarter to the ancient Arndale Market and the hip Mackie Mayor. Make easy use of this guide's current information, alluring images, and thorough maps to discover Manchester's vibrant food markets and street food hotspots. Explore the best of Manchester's food offerings in 2024 and beyond, and embrace the city's unique culinary diversity to make really memorable culinary experiences.

Chapter 4: Cultural Insights

Local Customs and Traditions

Gaining an understanding of Manchester's regional cultures and traditions enhances your trip and helps you establish a stronger bond with the locals. Manchester, a melting pot of cultures and a powerhouse of innovation, features a rich tapestry of traditions that reflect its historical background and modern vibrancy. In order to help you completely immerse yourself in the local culture during your stay in 2024 and beyond, this section of your indispensable guide delves into the distinctive practices and traditions that define Manchester. It is enhanced with current information, engaging images, and thorough maps.

Amicable Mancunian Essence

The kind and hospitable demeanour of Manchester's citizens, referred to as Mancunians, is among the city's most remarkable features. Tourists frequently comment on how approachable and pleasant the residents are; they take pride in their city and are always willing to lend a helping hand or strike up a conversation. Talking to locals can improve your experience by giving you insightful information about the history, culture, and way of life of the city. Never be afraid to start a conversation in pubs, cafes, or while taking in the various sights the city has to offer.

Football Enthusiasm

Manchester is known for its love of football, and it is home to two of the biggest teams in the world, Manchester United and Manchester City. This fierce rivalry is deeply ingrained in the local culture and identity and transcends beyond sports. When fans don their club colours and congregate in pubs, stadiums, and open viewing places to cheer for their teams, the city comes alive with excitement on match days. Sports fans must attend a game at either Old Trafford or the Etihad Stadium to get a sense of the passionate support and camaraderie that characterise Manchester's football culture.

Vast Musical Legacy

Manchester has made a significant contribution to the music industry by giving rise to legendary bands like The Smiths, Oasis, Joy Division, and The Stone Roses. Numerous live music venues, festivals, and historical locations honouring renowned musicians celebrate this rich musical legacy. The dynamic nightlife of the city, especially in neighbourhoods like Deansgate and the Northern Quarter, keeps a fertile ground for new musical talent and a wide range of musical styles. One can have a greater understanding of Manchester's ongoing impact on the world music scene by going to live performances or touring monuments associated with the music industry.

Bars and Conversation

The pub culture in Manchester is a vital aspect of social life, giving a pleasant and convivial setting where locals and visitors alike can unwind, chat, and enjoy a pint. In addition to being excellent locations to try regional beers and substantial pub meals, classic pubs like The Briton, The Marble Arch, and The Castle Hotel also act as community hubs where people congregate to celebrate occasions and exchange tales. Embracing the pub culture and making a few trips to these places will give you a better grasp of Manchester's social dynamics as well as some unforgettable experiences.

Festivals & Events

Manchester's diverse population and vibrant cultural scene are reflected in the multitude of festivals and events held there year-round. Important occurrences consist of:

- **Manchester International Festival**: A biennial occasion that draws global artists and spectators with avant-garde shows in dance, theatre, music, and visual arts.
- **Manchester Pride**: One of the biggest LGBTQ+ events in the United Kingdom, with a colourful procession, live acts, and a range of cultural events to celebrate inclusivity and diversity.
- **Happy Chinese New Year**: This festival, which is held in Chinatown, showcases Manchester's ethnic past with traditional dragon dances, fireworks, and a range of cultural acts.
- **Manchester Food and Drink Festival**: An incredible gourmet event showcasing the best of Manchester's culinary offerings, this festival brings together top chefs, food vendors, and drink specialists.

Attending these festivals is a special way to interact with the city's various populations and feel its vibrant energy.

Conventional Marketplaces

Manchester's classic markets, such Mackie Mayor and Arndale Market, are thriving hubs of the community's culture in addition to being fantastic locations to shop. These markets give visitors a flavour of Manchester life by offering a variety of handmade goods, street cuisine, and fresh vegetables. By visiting these markets, you may engage with neighbourhood merchants, taste some of the best cuisine from the area, and take in the vibrant energy that these well-liked public areas have to offer.

Honouring Our Heritage

Manchester is proud of its past, and it celebrates its heritage with a variety of customs and holidays. Landmarks like the Manchester Town Hall and the John Rylands Library are not only architectural marvels but also emblems of the city's enduring legacy. Annual activities such as the Whitworth Art Gallery's open days and guided historical tours offer insights into Manchester's past and its growth into a modern metropolis. Participating in these heritage festivals will help you appreciate the city's continuing progress as well as its illustrious past.

Honouring Regional Customs

Even though most Mancunians are warm and inviting, knowing and adhering to local customs and etiquette will improve your relationships. Typical courtesy includes:

- **Salutations**: When meeting someone for the first time, you should usually greet them with a grin and firm handshake.
- **In line**: Orderly lines are valued by Mancunians at bus stops, cafes, and retail establishments. Always be patient and wait your turn.
- **Giving**: If service is not included in the bill, it is common to give a tip in restaurants and cafes of approximately 10% to 15%.

Respecting the local culture and ensuring positive relationships are made easier by being aware of certain social conventions.

Visitors can enjoy a rich and engaging cultural experience with Manchester's cultures and traditions. The city's customs show its innovative and eclectic spirit, from the fervent football fans and lively musical legacy to the friendly pub culture and exciting festivals. You may make the most of your trip and forge deep bonds with Manchester's core by participating in these traditions and adhering to local manners. Make the most of this guide's current information, engrossing images, and thorough maps to explore and appreciate Manchester's distinctive cultural landscape and ensure an enriching and unforgettable trip through one of the UK's most vibrant towns in 2024 and beyond.

Festivals and Events

Manchester is a city full of life all year long, with a wide range of festivals and events honouring its lively arts scene, rich cultural heritage, and strong sense of community. Manchester caters to all interests and passions with events ranging from cutting edge food fairs and sports extravaganzas to world-class music festivals and vibrant cultural festivities. In order to help you organise your participation and completely immerse yourself in the festive spirit of the city, this section of your indispensable companion offers an overview of the must-attend festivals and events in Manchester for 2024, complete with up-to-date information, engaging images, and thorough maps.

Manchester International Festival

The Manchester International Festival (MIF), a biennial event that features cutting-edge performances in music, theatre, dance, and visual arts, is a mainstay of Manchester's cultural calendar. MIF, which is slated to happen in 2025, brings together well-known artists and up-and-coming creatives from all over the world to produce original and cutting-edge experiences. Expect a varied schedule that includes everything from cutting-edge musical performances and interactive displays to cutting-edge theatre productions and innovative art installations. This celebration of artistic brilliance is set against the appropriate backdrop provided by the festival venues, which include the landmark Manchester Central Convention Complex and the creative areas in the Northern Quarter. In order to guarantee entry to well-liked concerts and events, attendees can buy tickets online ahead of time.

Pride in Manchester

Manchester Pride is one of the biggest LGBTQ+ festivals in the UK, celebrating inclusiveness and diversity. This colourful event, which takes place in August every year, turns the city into a bright celebration of equality, love, and community. The magnificent Pride Parade, which takes place through Manchester's streets and draws thousands of participants and onlookers, is the main event. A variety of other events are also offered by the festival, such as drag shows, film screenings, art exhibits, and live music performances. Manchester Pride, which takes place mostly in the Gay Village along Canal Street, is known for its lively vibe and many bars, clubs, and other places that host activities all weekend long. One of the best ways to see the inclusive and vibrant side of the city is to take part in the parade and go to the numerous parties and shows.

Food and Drink Festival in Manchester

The Manchester Food and Drink Festival honours the city's varied culinary culture and is a must-attend event for foodies. This event, which is usually held in July, offers a delicious array of tastings, workshops, and demonstrations by bringing together top chefs, regional suppliers, and creative food vendors. Everything from excellent wines and craft breweries to artisanal cheeses and gourmet street cuisine is available for sampling by visitors. The festival is held in a number of sites throughout the city, such as the Manchester Central Convention Complex and Deansgate Locks, offering plenty of chances to sample local cuisine and discover new neighbourhoods. All guests will find the festival to be both entertaining and educational thanks to the interactive cooking courses and food-themed speeches that provide an educational element.

Street Art Festival Darnell

The Darnell Street Art Festival is a dynamic event that turns public places into bright canvases of street art and graffiti, reflecting Manchester's status as a hub for creativity and urban art. Every year, the vibrant Northern Quarter hosts the event, which draws international artists who participate in live painting workshops, interactive installations, and murals of significant size. It is possible for tourists to stroll about the streets, take in the vibrant artwork, and even take part in workshops where they may make their own works of street art. The festival encourages artistic expression and a sense of community in addition to beautifying the city. In addition to the visual art, food vendors and musical acts provide a lively and entertaining atmosphere suitable for all ages.

Winter Wonderland with Christmas Markets

Manchester welcomes the holiday season with its charming Christmas Markets and Winter Wonderland as the year comes to an end. These markets, which are usually hosted in late November and early December, turn the city centre into a wintry paradise complete with glistening lights, joyous décor, and quaint wooden kiosks. There is a large selection of handcrafted goods, seasonal fare, and festive drinks like hot chocolate and mulled wine available for visitors to peruse. Families, couples and friends will find the Winter Wonderland section to be a magical destination with its ice skating rinks, funfair attractions and live entertainment. The idyllic environment surrounding Deansgate Locks and Albert Square makes for a wonderful backdrop for holiday festivities and shopping.

Manchester Running Events & Marathon

The Manchester Marathon and related running events are the highlights of the city's sporting calendar for sports fans and active travellers. Every October, the marathon draws thousands of runners from across the globe with its tough and beautiful course that highlights Manchester's parks, landmarks, and lively neighbourhoods. It is an inclusive event for runners of all abilities because, in addition to the full marathon, there are other shorter events and fun runs that are tailored to different fitness levels. Along the route, spectators can support the participants while taking in the joyous atmosphere and sense of camaraderie that permeates the occasion. For those who want to be ready for the marathon, there are training sessions and running clinics that offer a motivating setting for fitness aficionados.

Manchester's thriving cultural scene, diverse population, and boundless inventiveness are all demonstrated by the city's festivals and events. There is always something fascinating going on in Manchester, whether you are drawn to the creative innovations of the Manchester International Festival, the vibrant celebrations of Manchester Pride, the gastronomic delights of the Food and Drink Festival, or the magical atmosphere of the Christmas Markets. Utilize the up-to-date information, engaging images, and precise maps in this book to organise your participation and make the most of these remarkable experiences. In 2024 and beyond, discover one of the UK's most vibrant and culturally diverse cities, Manchester. Soak up the vibrant energy of the city's festivals and events and make lifelong memories.

Art and Music Scene

Manchester, a city well-known for its industrial might and rich cultural legacy, has a thriving and dynamic music and art scene that draws in both residents and tourists. Manchester presents a diverse array of artistic expression, ranging from modern art galleries displaying masterpieces of contemporary art to renowned music venues that have given rise to iconic bands. With the help of beautiful photographs, up-to-date information, and thorough maps, this section of your indispensable guide dives deep into Manchester's cultural and musical landscape, enabling you to explore and fully immerse yourself in the city's creative scene in 2024 and beyond.

A Renowned Musical Heritage

Manchester has had a significant impact on the world music landscape since it gave rise to influential bands and musicians who have influenced many other genres. Punk and post-punk bands like Joy Division and The Fall rose to prominence in the 1970s, launching the city's musical journey and laying the groundwork for later movements. Britpop icons like The Smiths, Oasis, and The Stone Roses rose to prominence in the 1980s and 1990s, solidifying Manchester's standing as a global hub for musical creativity. This rich history is being preserved by modern artists who push the boundaries of their medium while finding inspiration in the city's legendary past.

Symbolic Music Locations

Some of the most recognisable music venues in the world can be found in Manchester; they all have their own distinct vibes and host a wide range of events. Remarkable musical experiences are offered by The Manchester Arena, one of the biggest indoor arenas in Europe that draws big touring artists and international superstars. The O2 Ritz, a landmark location renowned for its breathtaking Art Deco architecture, presents a range of live events from hip-hop and techno to rock and indie. Band on the Wall in the Northern Quarter, which promotes a close-knit community of music lovers, provides a cosy setting for live jazz, blues, and world music performances for those looking for something more private.

Vibrant Creative Spaces and Art Galleries

Manchester has a thriving art scene as well, with several galleries and creative spaces exhibiting both well-known and up-and-coming artists. The Whitworth is a premier art gallery that skilfully combines modern and historical design elements. Situated in Whitworth Park, the gallery showcases a remarkable assortment of fine art, textiles, and contemporary installations. It consistently organises avant-garde shows that provoke and motivate viewers. Leading venue for modern theatre, film, and art **HOME Manchester** offers a varied schedule of exhibitions, performances, and film screenings that showcase the artistic diversity of the city and offer a vibrant platform for creative expression.

Festivals and Live Music

The city's extensive roster of festivals and events demonstrates its dedication to live music. Manchester International Festival (MIF), held biennially, highlights cutting-edge performances and installations from global artists, creating a spirit of innovation and collaboration. In addition to honouring LGBTQ+ culture, Manchester Pride offers an exciting lineup of live musical acts that liven up the city's streets. Furthermore, the Manchester Food and Drink Festival combines live music with its celebration of delicious food to provide guests a multimodal experience. These occasions showcase Manchester's standing as a centre of culture, where the arts and music combine to produce captivating encounters.

Public artwork and street art

Beautiful murals and public art works line Manchester's streets, showcasing the city's artistic culture and appreciation of urban artwork. Street art abounds in the Northern Quarter, where bright canvases are painted on walls by both local and foreign artists. A combination of modern and traditional public art creates a visually exciting landscape that begs for investigation and appreciation in the Castlefield area. In addition to adding to the city's aesthetic appeal, these public artworks share tales of Manchester's inventive past and rich cultural legacy.

The Role of Education and Institutions

Manchester's artistic and musical potential is greatly aided by educational institutions. Both Manchester Metropolitan University and The Royal Northern College of Music (RNCM) are well-known for their demanding curricula and contributions to the creative industries. These schools turn forth talented musicians, performers, and artists who keep enhancing Manchester's cultural landscape. University-local gallery collaborations and joint initiatives provide a dynamic intellectual exchange that keeps Manchester at the forefront of creative and musical innovation.

Local Bands and Artists

The vitality of Manchester's creative environment is derived from its local bands and artists, who consistently push boundaries and redefine genres. While indie favourites like The Courteeners and Gibbons Folk continue to enjoy a devoted local following, up-and-coming artists like Everything Everything and The 1975 have received international acclaim. Artists can experiment and flourish in a setting that encourages artistic expression and innovation because to the city's support of community-based music and art programs.

Advice for Appreciating Music and Art in Manchester

- **Explore Diverse Venues**: Manchester has a variety of venues to fit every taste, from large arenas to small clubs and unique galleries. To truly enjoy the wide range of artistic offerings available in the city, take some time to explore various spaces.

- **Remain Up to Date on Events**: For information on live concerts, gallery openings, and festivals, check your local listings and event calendars. It is best to get tickets in advance for well-attended events.

- **Participate in the Community**: Take part in interactive exhibitions, seminars, and workshops to get a deeper understanding of Manchester's music and art scene. These events create deep relationships with regional creatives and offer insightful information.

- **Support Local Talent**: To help up-and-coming musicians and artists, check out independent galleries and neighbourhood music venues. Your purchases support the thriving creative ecosystem in Manchester.

Manchester's thriving music and art scenes are a testament to the city's inventive spirit and rich cultural legacy. Manchester provides a plethora of creative activities to suit every taste, whether you are taking in live performances at historic venues, exploring modern art galleries, or losing yourself in the echoes of legendary bands. Make the most of this guide's current information, gorgeous pictures, and thorough maps to explore and fully appreciate the city's vibrant musical and creative scene. Explore the rhythms and hues that make Manchester unique, and let the creative energy of the city to motivate you as you travel across one of the most fascinating and culturally diverse places in the UK in 2024 and beyond.

Chapter 5: Essential Tips and Laws

Important Travel Tips

Considering a vacation to Manchester? Being well-prepared is crucial to guaranteeing a hassle-free, pleasurable, and seamless visit. Manchester is a thriving city with a wealth of activities for all kinds of tourists. It is renowned for its lively culture, rich history, and active lifestyle. This section of your essential companion contains critical travel recommendations, enhanced with up-to-date information, practical guidance, and thorough maps to help you navigate and make the most of your Manchester experience in 2024 and beyond.

Currency and Payments

Manchester uses the British Pound Sterling (£) as its currency. Although most places in the city accept credit and debit cards, it is a good idea to have some cash on hand for smaller businesses, street markets, and unexpected situations. There are lots of ATMs and many of them allow contactless withdrawals. Furthermore, mobile payment services like Google Wallet and Apple Pay are becoming more and more well-liked since they offer safe and practical means to conduct transactions. To effectively manage your spending, think about purchasing a prepaid travel card if you intend to visit several sites or eat at several places.

Travel Advice

Manchester has a robust public transport system that makes getting about the city and its environs simple. The core of Manchester's public transportation network is the Metrolink tram system, which links important locations like the city centre, Manchester Airport, Salford Quays, and significant neighbourhoods. The tram network is enhanced by buses, which provide regular and extensive service. For longer journeys or day visits, Manchester Piccadilly Station provides excellent rail connections to destinations like London, Liverpool, Leeds, and Edinburgh.

If you intend to use public transport frequently, investing in a day ticket or weekly travelcard will help you save money and traverse the city more effectively. In addition, Santander Cycles, Manchester's public bike-sharing program, is one of the many bike-friendly rental alternatives and bike lanes in the city. Many of Manchester's attractions are accessible by foot for those who choose to travel that way, especially in the city centre and its environs.

Security and Safety

Although Manchester is a fairly secure city for tourists, it is still advisable to exercise caution as with any large city. Watch out for your possessions, particularly in busy areas like marketplaces, public transportation, and tourist destinations. Refrain from flaunting expensive things and use caution when accessing ATMs. Emergency services can be obtained by dialing 999 or 112 for police, fire, or medical assistance.

Spoken Word and Verbal Exchange

Since English is the official language in Manchester, communicating with visitors who speak it is simple. But, because Manchester is a multinational city with a varied population, you can run into people speaking different languages and accents. Although knowing a few simple British English phrases will improve your communication, there are not many language obstacles in general.

Atmosphere and Apparel

Manchester is well-known for its erratic weather, which is frequently marked by sporadic downpours. It seems sense to include layers, such as a walking shoe that fits well and a waterproof jacket. Even in the summer, evenings can get chilly, so it is a good idea to pack a lightweight jacket or jumper. To ensure that you are comfortable when touring the city, check the weather prediction ahead of time and pack accordingly for changing conditions.

Reservations for Lodging

Manchester provides a wide selection of accommodation alternatives to suit every budget and preference, from luxurious hotels and romantic bed-and-breakfasts to budget-friendly hostels and serviced apartments. Making reservations in advance guarantees you get the greatest deals and your first choice of places, especially during busy travel seasons and important events. Consider staying in central locations like the Northern Quarter, Deansgate, or Salford Quays for convenient access to sights, restaurants, and nightlife.

Regional Traditions and Protocols

It can improve your travel experience and promote favourable relationships with locals if you are aware of the norms and etiquette. Mancunian kindness and civility are well-known. Grinning when you welcome someone, queuing politely, and honouring personal space are common courtesies. In pubs and restaurants, it's traditional to give a tip of roughly 10-15% if service is not included in the bill. When you visit places of worship, dress modestly and treat others with respect.

Emergency Numbers and Medical Information

Make sure you have access to crucial contact details while you are visiting. For immediate assistance, dial 999 or 112 in the UK. The National Health Service (NHS) offers full healthcare services for non-emergency medical needs. It is advised to purchase travel insurance to cover any unanticipated medical costs or emergencies.

Internet and connectivity

Manchester has many places to stay connected, including public areas, hotels, and cafes. If you will be using your travel phone for calls and dependable mobile data, think about getting a local SIM card. Prepaid choices with different data bundles are available from major providers such as EE, Vodafone, and O2 to meet your needs.

Visitor Information Desks

There are a number of tourist information centres in Manchester where you can pick up brochures, maps, and tailored travel tips. The primary hub is situated close to Manchester Piccadilly Station, while other hubs are situated at strategic sites such Salford Quays and the Manchester Central Convention Complex. These hubs are a great place to look up the greatest places to eat, see the latest events, and activities.

Usability

Manchester is dedicated to providing equal access to its city for every visitor. Trams, buses and trains are examples of public transportation choices that have amenities for people with mobility impairments, such as low-floor trams and step-free access at stations. Additionally, a lot of hotels, eateries, and activities offer accessible amenities. It is best to get in touch with venues ahead of time if you need special accommodations to make sure your demands are satisfied.

Packing List Essentials

To guarantee a pleasant and enjoyable journey, consider bringing the following essentials:

- **Travel documents**: Passport, visa (if applicable), travel insurance, and lodging confirmations.
- **Apparel**: Seasonal wear, walking shoes that are comfortable, a waterproof jacket, and layers of clothes.
- **Electronics**: portable battery pack, charger, power adaptor (UK plugs are Type G), smartphone.
- **Personal items**: a small umbrella, reusable water bottle, prescriptions, and toiletries.
- **Other items**: maps, travel guide, and a compact daypack for outings.

Manchester is a city full of opportunities, with a diverse range of historical, cultural, and contemporary attractions. You can make the most of your trip and traverse the city with confidence if you heed these crucial travel advices. Make use of the most recent data, useful suggestions, and thorough maps found in this book to guarantee a smooth and unforgettable trip through one of the most vibrant and hospitable cities in the UK in 2024 and beyond. Savour the distinctive experiences Manchester has to offer and make lasting memories while you are there.

Safety and Health Information

Enjoying everything Manchester has to offer when visiting is contingent upon ensuring your safety and well-being. Like any big city, Manchester is generally a safe and friendly place to visit, but it is still advisable to be aware and take the appropriate safety measures. To guarantee a safe and healthy visit to Manchester in 2024 and beyond, this section of your indispensable companion offers comprehensive safety and health information, enhanced with current details, useful advice, and handy maps.

Overall Safety Advice

Although Manchester is thought to be a secure travel destination, you may increase your security by being aware of your surroundings and taking sensible precautions:

- **Remain Vigilant**: Pay attention to your surroundings, particularly when you are in crowded places like marketplaces, bus stops, and tourist attractions. Pickpocketing and small-time stealing are common, especially in crowded areas.

- **Protect Your Property**: Carry zippered bags and wear them close to your body. Steer clear of overtly flaunting expensive stuff like jewellery, cameras, and cellphones.

- **Steer clear of isolated and dark areas**: Even though Manchester is safe, it is best to stay away from dimly lit, empty streets after dark. Remain in crowded, well-trafficked places, particularly after dark.

- **Use Reputable Transportation**: Choose ride-sharing services such as Uber or authorised taxis. When on public transportation, keep your distance from other patrons and use caution with your possessions.

- **Contacts for Emergencies**: Learn the local emergency numbers by heart. In the UK, in case of a police, fire, or medical emergency, contact 999 or 112.

Contacts for Emergencies

Having access to critical contact information is crucial in case of emergencies:

- **Emergency Services**: To get police, fire, or medical assistance right away, dial 999 or 112.

- **Non-Emergency Police**: Call the Greater Manchester Police at 101 for non-urgent police problems.

- **British Red Cross**: Call their helpline or visit their website for information and support.

- **Hospitals in the Area**: Learn the locations of the hospitals in your area. Christie Hospital, Wythenshawe Hospital, and Manchester Royal Infirmary are some of the city's major medical facilities.

Medical Institutions

Manchester has a strong healthcare system that guarantees guests may get medical attention when needed:

- **NHS Services**: Both locals and visitors can receive complete medical care from the National Health Service (NHS). You could be able to receive NHS care if you are a citizen of the EU or if you possess the necessary visa. Having your European Health Insurance Card (EHIC) or similar documents on you is advised.
- **Secure Medical Care**: Fast-track medical treatments are available at many hospitals and private clinics. The Christie and Nuffield Health Manchester are two examples of facilities that

offer a variety of medical services and consultations.

- **Medicines**: Manchester has a large number of pharmacies that provide prescription drugs, over-the-counter pharmaceuticals, and health advice. Common chains in the city are Lloyds Pharmacy and Boots.

Insurance for Travel

It is strongly advised to purchase comprehensive travel insurance to protect against unforeseen medical expenses, theft, accidents, and cancelled trips. Make sure the following is covered by your policy:

- **Medical Coverage:** Includes emergency medical care, doctor visits, and hospital stays.
- **Personal Liability:** Guards against lawsuits should you unintentionally hurt someone else or damage someone else's property.
- **Trip Interruption:** Covers non-refundable costs in the event that unanticipated events force you to cancel your trip.

- **Lost or Stolen Belongings**: Offers reimbursement for misplaced, pilfered, or harmed personal property.

COVID-19 and Health Care for All

COVID-19 protocols may have changed by 2024, however it is still important to stay up to date on the most recent public health recommendations:

- **vaccines**: Before departing, make sure you have received all advised vaccines. Verify whether any particular vaccines are needed in order to enter.

- **Health Guidelines**: Pay attention to local health recommendations about wearing masks, keeping social distance, and maintaining good hygiene, particularly when using public transportation and in crowded areas.

- **Testing and Quarantine**: Keep yourself updated about any testing requirements or quarantine procedures that may apply to travellers, especially in the event that international health conditions change.

Municipal Rules and Laws

It is imperative to comprehend and abide by local laws and regulations to ensure a trouble-free visit:
- **Drinking Age**: In the UK, the legal drinking age is eighteen. Although it is usually okay to drink in public, there could be certain limitations in place.
- **Smoking**: It is not permitted to smoke in any enclosed public area, including eateries, pubs and public transportation. Certain outdoor locations have spaces specifically designated for smoking.
- **Drug Laws**: Illegal drug possession, usage, and trafficking are all rigorously forbidden and carry stiff penalties, including jail time.
- **Public Behaviour**: It is expected that one behaves respectfully in public areas. Vandalism and loud noises are examples of public disorder acts that can result in penalties or legal action.

Usability

Manchester is dedicated to being a welcoming destination for all tourists, making sure that those with impairments or other mobility issues can pleasantly enjoy their stay:

- **Public Transportation**: Low-floor trams, step-free station access and priority seating on buses are just a few of the amenities available to people with mobility impairments using the Metrolink tram, bus and train system.

- **Accessible Venues**: A lot of tourist destinations, lodging options, dining establishments, and open areas are made to be accessible. It is a good idea to look at accessibility features when making travel or hotel arrangements, especially when visiting certain locations.

- **Services of Assistance**: To make sure your needs can be met, get in touch with the venue or service provider ahead of time if you need any special assistance.

Maintaining Your Health

Keeping yourself healthy whilst travelling is crucial to a good trip:

- **Keep Yourself Hydrated:** Because of Manchester's variable weather, it is important to stay hydrated, especially if you want to be outside.
- **Balanced Diet:** Take advantage of Manchester's varied culinary scene, but make sure you consume meals that are balanced to keep your energy levels up.
- **Relaxation and Rest:** Take frequent pauses to unwind and revitalise, particularly if you are seeing a lot of the city.
- **Exercise:** To keep active while visiting Manchester, make use of the city's parks and outdoor areas for brisk walks or mild exercise.

Manchester is a friendly, safe city that provides visitors with a multitude of experiences. You may guarantee a safe and pleasurable visit by adhering to these health and safety recommendations, learning about local laws, and making enough preparations. Make the most of this guide's current information, useful suggestions, and thorough maps to explore Manchester with assurance and concentrate on making treasured moments in one of the UK's most vibrant and culturally diverse cities in 2024 and beyond. Savour the lively atmosphere of the city while keeping your security and wellbeing first, and take advantage of everything Manchester has to offer without worrying about anything.

Local Laws and Regulations

Comprehending and honouring Manchester's laws and ordinances is crucial for a trouble-free and delightful vacation. Although Manchester is a friendly and safe city overall, knowing the laws can help you move around with confidence and prevent any unintentional offences. This section of your indispensable guide offers a thorough summary of the most important local rules and ordinances, enhanced with current data, helpful tips, and thorough maps to ensure that you are knowledgeable and compliant when visiting Manchester in 2024 and beyond.

Drinking Alcohol

- **Aged Legally to Drink:** In Manchester, eighteen is the legal drinking age. This holds true for both buying and drinking alcohol in public and private settings. Pubs, taverns, and restaurants are among the establishments that closely monitor ID compliance.

- **Accredited Location:** Alcohol can only be drunk in licensed places, such as pubs, bars, and restaurants. It is usually forbidden to consume alcohol in public areas such as parks, streets, or on public transportation. Violations of this rule may result in penalties or the confiscation of alcohol by law enforcement.

- **Intoxicated Driver Laws:** The UK has severe regulations against drunk driving. The blood alcohol content (BAC) level is 0.08% legally, however it is just 0.02% for drivers under 25 or those with less than three years of driving experience. Police use breathalyser testing on a daily basis, and violators face harsh punishments include fines, license suspension, and jail time. If you have had alcohol, it is safest not to drive.

Smoking Laws

- **No Smoking in Public**: All enclosed public areas, such as restaurants, bars, public transportation, and workplaces, are smoke-free zones. Some outdoor places, including some pubs and event spaces, have designated smoking zones.
- **Electronic cigarettes**: Similar regulations apply to e-cigarette usage as they do to regular smoking. In enclosed public venues and businesses, they are not allowed; however, they are typically allowed in specified outside locations.
- **Age Restrictions**: It takes 18 years of age to legally purchase tobacco goods. Tobacco sales to minors are strictly prohibited, and retailers are compelled to verify identification.

Laws Concerning Drugs

- **Illicit narcotics**: It is absolutely forbidden to possess, consume, or deal in illegal narcotics in

Manchester or the rest of the United Kingdom. Heavy penalties, incarceration, and a criminal record are among the consequences. The government imposes strict enforcement of these prohibitions, conducting frequent police operations aimed at drug-related activity.

- **Medications on Prescription**: If you need prescription drugs, be sure you have a legitimate prescription and the drugs in their original packaging. Consult your healthcare professional prior to travel as some medications that are permitted in other nations may not be allowed in the UK.

Disorder and Public Behaviour

- **Public Order Offenses**: Laws are in place to punish acts of public disorder, which include loud noises, vandalism, and hostile conduct. Remaining polite in public areas is crucial to avoiding fines or getting arrested.
- **Coat Codes**: Even though Manchester is a multicultural and accepting city, there may be

dress codes at some establishments, especially upscale dining establishments and clubs. To guarantee entrance, it is a good idea to confirm the particular requirements of the places you intend to visit.

- **Laws of Photography**: In general, taking pictures in public spaces is permitted, however there are limitations in some locations, including government facilities, military installations, and private homes. Before taking a picture of someone, you should always get their consent, especially in private or delicate situations.

Road and Traffic Laws

- **Manchester driving**: Keep in mind that the UK drives on the left side of the road if you intend to drive in Manchester. Make sure your driver's license is up to date that you understand all applicable local traffic laws, such as those pertaining to parking and speed limits.

- **Parking Guidelines**: Manchester has very tight parking laws, particularly in the downtown area.

Observe any signage pertaining to parking zones, regulations, and costs. To locate available spots and stay out of trouble, use parking applications or park-and-ride facilities.

- **Laws governing cycling**: Manchester has many bike lanes and is a bike-friendly city. Road laws must be followed by cyclists, who also have to use lights at night and wear helmets. Make sure your bicycle has all the safety features required to meet local laws.

Honouring Regional Traditions and Etiquette

- **Queuing**: Patients and neat lines are important to the people of Munich. When in queue for services such as shops or public transport, always wait your turn with patience.
- **Sipping Customs**: Tipping is expected in cafes, restaurants, and bars; if service is not included, it is usually between 10% and 15% of the total price. It is valued as a thank-you gift for excellent service.

- **Dignity with Honour**: Manchester is an inclusive city that values variety. Respect other people's cultures, faiths, and ways of life to promote harmony and constructive interactions.

Emergency Support and Services

- **Emergency Contacts**: To contact law enforcement, firefighters, or emergency medical services, dial 999 or 112. These numbers are helpful to have stored on your phone or written down in your travel documents.
- **Medical Facilities in the Area**: Manchester offers first-rate medical facilities, including both private and NHS clinics. Know where the closest hospitals, such Christie Hospital or Manchester Royal Infirmary, are located in case you need medical attention.

Respecting and being knowledgeable of Manchester's local laws and regulations will improve your trip and guarantee a trouble-free stay. You may take full advantage of everything

Manchester has to offer while remaining safe and compliant by reading and following these rules. In 2024 and beyond, navigate the city's legal environment with confidence by using the most recent information, useful tips, and thorough maps provided in this guide. This will free up your time to concentrate on creating unforgettable experiences in one of the UK's most vibrant and culturally diverse places. Accept Manchester's lively culture while adhering to its laws, and take pleasure in a smooth and pleasurable travel around this amazing city.

Conclusion

Recap of Highlights

Manchester, a vibrant, creative city, offers a unique fusion of culture, history, and contemporary innovation. Manchester promises a rich and varied experience that appeals to every interest, whether you are visiting for the first time or coming back to explore more. As your vital companion, this guide has introduced you to the numerous features that make Manchester a must-visit place in 2024 and beyond. Let's revisit the attractions that await you in this bustling Northern England city.

Historical Sites and Famous Landmarks

Manchester's history is closely linked to the Industrial Revolution, and the city is delighted to display its legacy through magnificent buildings and conserved sites. The magnificent Victorian Gothic Revival Manchester Town Hall is a reminder of the affluent history of the city. The magnificent neo-Gothic John Rylands Library holds rare volumes and manuscripts that provide insight into the city's rich intellectual history. Manchester Cathedral and Chetham's Library, the oldest public library in the English-speaking world, further enrich your trip through time, giving calm sanctuaries and architectural grandeur.

World-Class Galleries and Museums

Manchester's galleries and museums are a must-visit for everyone interested in art and history. Natural history, fine art, and contemporary installations are all featured in the vast collections of The Manchester Museum and The Whitworth art gallery. The Lowry at Salford Quays reflects the industrial heritage of the city by fusing performances with an amazing exhibition of L.S. Lowry's well-known artwork. For more in-depth study of science and technology, check out the Science and Industry Museum, which features historical artefacts and interactive exhibitions honouring Manchester's crucial role in invention.

Dynamic Scene of Music and Art

Manchester has earned its standing as a major cultural hub, especially when it comes to music and art. Famous bands like The Smiths, Oasis, and Joy Division were formed in the city, and its music venues, like The O2 Ritz and Band on the Wall, still stage live concerts that preserve the city's musical heritage. Places like HOME Manchester, a hub for modern theatre, cinema, and art, and the Northern Quarter, dotted with vibrant street art and independent galleries, are great places to see art. Manchester is kept at the forefront of artistic innovation and expression thanks to these creative hubs.

Varied Culinary Adventures

Manchester's culinary culture, which offers a mouthwatering variety of cuisines and dining experiences, is a reflection of its diversified population. The city offers something for every taste, from foreign cuisine in Rusholme Curry Mileto classic British fare at historic pubs like Albert's Schloss. Food markets such as Arndale Market and Mackie Mayor feature a diverse mix of street food sellers, allowing you to try everything from gourmet burgers to exotic Middle Eastern cuisine. Restaurants such as Australasia and The Refuge by Volta provide creative menus that combine regional ingredients with international flavours for a more sophisticated dining experience.

Generous Parks and Green Areas
Manchester has a lot of parks and outdoor areas that provide a break from the bustle of the city despite its metropolitan setting. One of Europe's biggest municipal parks, Heaton Park has wide lawns, picturesque lakes, and landmarks dating back to the 1800s like Heaton Hall. With its themed gardens and abundant flora, Fletcher Moss Botanical Garden in Didsbury provides a peaceful

haven, and Whitworth Park The Whitworth gallery blends modern architecture with the natural world. Families and lovers of the outdoors will find lots to enjoy in these green spaces, which are ideal for leisurely walks, picnics, and outdoor activities.

Intense Celebrations and Occasions

Manchester's calendar is jam-packed with celebrations of its lively community spirit and diverse culture, including festivals and events. Manchester Pride celebrates diversity with a vibrant parade and a variety of cultural events, while the Manchester International Festival features cutting-edge performances and installations by international artists. Sports fans may enjoy the excitement of the Manchester Marathon and foodies can indulge in the Manchester Food and Drink Festival. These gatherings not only showcase the vibrant character of the city but also offer chances to interact with its hospitable and diverse populace.

Useful Travel Advice

Manchester's large public transport network, which includes the Metrolink tram network and several bus lines, makes getting about easy. Staying in the Northern Quarter or Salford Quays puts you in close proximity to all the major sights, restaurants, and nightlife the area has to offer. Understanding local customs, such as queuing etiquette and tipping practices, enhances your interactions with locals and assures a courteous and pleasurable vacation. You may also explore the city with peace of mind if you prioritise safety by being alert of your surroundings and protecting your valuables.

Manchester is a city of contrasts and harmony, where historical charm meets modern innovation, and cultural variety produces a lively and welcoming environment. With its renowned buildings, top-notch museums, vibrant art and music scene, varied gastronomic options, and large green areas, Manchester has a lot to offer visitors of all interests. Make the most of this guide's current information, gorgeous pictures, and thorough maps to explore and experience everything Manchester has to offer. In 2024 and beyond, embrace the vibrant energy of the city and make lifelong memories while visiting one of the most fascinating and culturally diverse places in the UK. Greetings from Manchester, where each visit promises to be an exciting new journey.

Encouragement for Exploration

Manchester's diverse experiences, lively neighbourhoods, and plenty of hidden jewels entice inquisitive people and reward the daring. Manchester provides countless options for discovery, whether you choose to explore through its historic streets, explore its modern art scenes, or indulge in its varied culinary offerings. This portion of your indispensable companion invites you to stray from the beaten route and thoroughly experience what makes this city so alluring in 2024 and beyond.

Accept the Neighbours

Finding the various neighbourhoods in Manchester, each with its own unique personality and charm, is one of the best things about visiting the city. In the centre of the city, you may begin your adventure amid the busy Arndale Market and Manchester Town Hall, two classic structures that combine with contemporary shopping areas and lively street life. Explore the Northern Quarter from here, which is renowned for its bohemian atmosphere, unique shops, eccentric cafés, and breathtaking street art. This area is great for individuals who enjoy to explore on foot, with narrow lanes and unique places around every turn.

Travel west to Salford Quays, a waterfront neighbourhood that was formerly industrial docks but is now a thriving cultural centre. Here, you may visit The Lowry, attend a performance at

HOME Manchester, or simply stroll along the gorgeous promenade, taking in views of the River Irwell and the spectacular media skyline. Each district offers a unique slice of Manchester's diverse personality, enabling you to explore and find what resonates most with you.

Find Undiscovered Treasures

Beyond the big attractions, Manchester is packed with hidden jewels waiting to be unearthed. Stroll slowly around Castlefield, where modern bars and calm waterways coexist with the remains of an ancient Roman settlement. This region offers a peaceful respite from the bustle of the city, seamlessly fusing history and contemporary. Discover Manchester's industrial history by visiting the Museum of Science and Industry. Alternatively, take a picturesque boat ride or a leisurely stroll along the Bridgewater Canal.

Quieter areas like Chorlton and Didsbury are home to charming small stores, quaint taverns, and parks. For those looking to escape the bustle of the city, these neighbourhoods provide a more laid-back pace and a window into the daily lives of Manchester residents.

Get Involved in Local Culture

Manchester's robust cultural scene is a monument to its diverse and welcoming community. Participate in community activities and workshops, see live music performances in small venues, or interact with local artists in pop-up galleries and street exhibitions. The vibrant arts sector in the city is ever-changing, providing citizens with new and inventive experiences that are a reflection of their creative spirit.

Do not pass up the chance to talk to residents and learn insider information on the best-kept secrets of the city. Engaging in social interactions at a café, going on a passionate Manchester resident's guided tour, or going to a community festival can all help you better comprehend and value Manchester's distinctive cultural environment.

Savour the Variety of Cuisines

Manchester boasts an eclectic food culture, which makes discovering it one of the most thrilling experiences. Go beyond classic British cuisine and savour a variety of foreign dishes that showcase the diverse population of the city. Manchester's culinary culture is an incredible culinary journey, offering everything from traditional Indian fare on the Curry Mile to creative fusion delicacies in the Northern Quarter.

Discover markets where you may enjoy a range of street food sellers selling everything from gourmet burgers to unique Asian specialities, such as Mackie Mayor and Arndale Market. For foodies wishing to sample the finest of Manchester's culinary choices in one handy place, these lively markets are ideal.

Make Use of the Effective Transit

Manchester's extensive public transport network makes it simple and hassle-free to explore the city's various areas. You can easily navigate the city and get to even the most isolated sights thanks to the Metrolink tram network, substantial bus services, and easy train linkages. You may explore Manchester at your own leisure by renting a bike or just going for a stroll, finding unexpected gems and hidden corners along the way.

Veer Away from the Trap

While Manchester's famous sites are absolutely worth visiting, venturing off the beaten path can lead to some of the most unforgettable encounters. Discover obscure museums, go to underground music venues, or find quiet parks and gardens that provide a respite from the bustling streets of the city. These distinct encounters offer a closer bond with Manchester's genuine and complex personality.

Manchester is a city rich in history, culture, and contemporary innovation that lives on exploration and discovery. You may design a unique and memorable experience by embracing the varied neighbourhoods, finding hidden jewels, interacting with the local way of life, indulging in delectable cuisine, and venturing off the main path. Utilize the up-to-date information, breathtaking images, and precise maps in this book to navigate Manchester comfortably and fully immerse yourself in all that this lively city has to offer. Follow your curiosity and set out on an exploration tour that will leave you with priceless memories and a profound respect for one of the liveliest and friendliest cities in the UK.

Bonus Section

Useful Apps for Travelers

The appropriate smartphone apps can greatly improve your Manchester travel experience in this digital age. These must-have applications are an indispensable resource for every visitor, helping them with everything from utilising the vast public transportation system to finding the greatest restaurants and maintaining connectivity. The must-have applications for exploring Manchester in 2024 are highlighted in this section of your indispensable companion. These apps come with useful advice, current information, and easy-to-use features to make sure your trip is seamless and pleasurable.

1. The Greater Manchester Transport Authority (TfGM) App

With the TfGM App, navigating Manchester's public transport system is a breeze. With the aid of this official software, you may effectively plan

your travels by getting real-time information on trains, buses, and trams. Features consist of:
- **Live Timetables**: Receive the most recent information on bus and tram schedules.
- **Route Planning**: With step-by-step instructions, quickly determine the optimal paths between locations.
- **Ticket Purchases**: Get your tickets online and store them there to avoid using paper ones.
- **Service Alerts**: Stay informed while on the go by receiving information about delays, cancellations, and changes to the service.

2. Maps by Google

Travellers still find Google Maps to be an essential tool due to its extensive mapping and navigation functions.
- **Detailed Maps**: Get access to comprehensive maps of Manchester that show bike and pedestrian paths.

- **Public Transportation Integration**: See schedules and available routes directly from the app.
- **Offline Maps**: Save maps to your device so you can navigate even when you do not have internet access.
- **Local Business Information**: Use user reviews and ratings to find local eateries, retail establishments, and points of interest.

3. Citymapper

Citymapper is a great option for people looking for a substitute for Google Maps, especially for public transit:

- **Multi-Modal Directions**: To determine the quickest route, combine walking, cycling, buses, trains, and trams.
- **Updates in Real Time**: Get up-to-date information about service interruptions and transport timetables.

- **Cost Comparison**: To make well-informed travel decisions, compare the costs and times of various transportation options.
- **Personalised Commutes**: Save and get alerts about your preferred routes.

4. Using TripAdvisor

Boost your sightseeing and food experiences with TripAdvisor:

- **Restaurant Reviews**: Find Manchester's best eateries, coffee shops, and street food vendors with thorough reviews and ratings.
- **Attraction Recommendations**: Based on user reviews, identify must-see historical places, museums, and attractions.
- **Booking Options**: Use the app to book tables at well-liked restaurants and buy tickets directly for attractions.
- **Travel Forums**: Participate in conversations with other travellers, offer advice, and discuss your experiences.

5. Make a table open

In Manchester, OpenTable guarantees that you never miss a reservation when dining:

- **Restaurants Reservations**: Reserve seats at a variety of eateries, including casual and fine dining establishments.
- **Menu Previews**: Examine menus ahead of time to determine your preferred dining location.
- **Special Requests**: Let us know about any dietary restrictions or preferred seating arrangements.
- **Real-Time Availability**: To save your position as soon as possible, check the availability of tables in real-time.

6. Bolt and Uber

The following are necessary for dependable and convenient transportation: Uber and Bolt

- **Ride-Hailing Services**: Select from a variety of vehicle options to fit your needs and easily schedule rides with a few taps.

- **Transparent Pricing**: Check fare estimates prior to making a reservation to efficiently manage your vacation budget.
- **Safety Features**: Track your ride in real-time for extra security and share trip data with friends and family.
- **Cashless Payments**: Use the app to conveniently pay using the method of your choice.

7. Make Manchester App Visit

Designed with travellers in mind, the official Visit Manchester App provides a plethora of resources and information:

- **Event Listings**: Keep track of forthcoming celebrations, exhibitions, and events taking place throughout the city.
- **Itinerary Planner**: Make customised itineraries according to your preferences and free time.
- **Special Offers**: Take advantage of extra savings and promotions on activities, meals, and lodging.

- **Interactive Maps**: Examine interactive maps that showcase important locations, such as well-known hotspots and hidden treasures.

8. Exchange Rate

You can easily manage your foreign exchange using the XE Currency app:

Get accurate and current exchange rates for the British Pound and other currencies with Real-Time Exchange Rates.

- **Currency Converter**: Convert prices quickly and see how much products and services cost in your native currency.

- **Alerts Regarding Rates**: To ensure that your currency conversion decisions are well-informed, set alerts for favourable exchange rates.

9. WhatsApp Enterprise and WhatsApp

Use WhatsApp to stay in touch with friends, family, and nearby companies.

- **Messaging and Calls:** Make audio and video calls using mobile data or Wi-Fi, as well as send instant messages.
- **Group conversations:** Use group conversations to arrange plans with fellow travellers.
- **WhatsApp Business:** Use the app to communicate directly with nearby companies for bookings, support, and questions.

10. Check Out Manchester's Social Networks

Keeping up with Manchester's official social media accounts available through a variety of apps keeps you updated on the newest events:

- **Facebook and Instagram:** Peruse the breathtaking images, event details, and insider advice provided by the city's tourism board.
- **Twitter:** Receive news, updates, and prompt answers to your questions about the city in real time.

If you have these must-have apps on your smartphone, visiting Manchester will be easy, productive, and enjoyable. These tools will improve every part of your trip, from using public transit and finding the finest places to eat to staying connected and aware of upcoming activities. Make use of these applications' current information, useful features, and intuitive user interfaces to explore Manchester with comfort and confidence. In 2024 and beyond, embrace the ease of contemporary technology and use these apps to be your dependable travel companions as you make lifelong memories in one of the most vibrant and hospitable cities in the UK.

Recommended Day Trips from Manchester

While Manchester has a lot to offer in terms of sights and activities, getting outside the city will reveal some of the most quaint and scenic locations in Northern England. These suggested day trips from Manchester provide a variety of interesting experiences, whether you are looking to explore old towns, take in breathtaking natural settings, or fully immerse yourself in cultural heritage. This section of your indispensable companion showcases the best places for day trips, enhanced with current data, gorgeous images, and comprehensive maps to assist you in organising your travels for 2024 and beyond.

Peak District National Park

The Peak District National Park is a must-visit for outdoor enthusiasts and wildlife lovers, and it is just under an hour's drive from Manchester. The park is well-known for its stunning scenery, which includes undulating hills, striking cliffs, tranquil valleys, and charming villages. Popular activities include hiking, cycling, rock climbing, and wildlife spotting. Famous locations like Mam Tor, renowned for its breathtaking panoramic vistas, and Stanage Edge, a favourite among climbers, offer incredible outdoor experiences. little towns like Bakewell, known for its infamous Bakewell pudding, and Castleton, with its magnificent Peveril Castle and picturesque caverns, are lovely places to explore regional cuisine and culture. Because of the Peak District's varied landscape, it is the perfect place to get away from the hustle and bustle of the city and unwind.

Liverpool

Liverpool, a thriving city rich in maritime history, musical legacy, and cultural variety, is only a short rail trip from Manchester. Liverpool, well-known for being the birthplace of The Beatles, has a lot to offer music lovers, including The Beatles Story Museum and the Cavern Club, where the iconic band practiced their trade. The Merseyside Maritime Museum and the International Slavery Museum, which offer illuminating historical viewpoints, are located near the Albert Dock, which highlights the city's strong maritime legacy. Art lovers will enjoy the Walker Art Gallery, which has a large collection of fine art, and the Tate Liverpool, which holds exhibitions of modern and contemporary art. Liverpool is a vibrant city ideal for a day of amusement and discovery because of its bustling markets, vibrant waterfront, and varied food scene.

Chester

Chester, a historic city with well-preserved Roman walls, mediaeval architecture, and quaint Tudor-style houses, is about an hour's drive from Manchester. Because of its small size, the city is ideal for a leisurely day excursion, with plenty of places to see on foot. Highlights include the majestic Chester Cathedral, the distinctive Chester Rows a unique collection of two-tiered medieval shopping galleries and the well-preserved Roman Amphitheatre, the largest in Britain. For sweeping views of Chester and the surrounding countryside, stroll along the city walls. Alternatively, enjoy a boat ride down the scenic River Dee. For both history enthusiasts and casual visitors, Chester's blend of modern conveniences and old history makes for an enthralling encounter.

York

If you are looking for a longer day trip, you may spend roughly two hours by rail from Manchester to the mediaeval city of York. York is famous for the mediaeval Shambles, a tiny cobblestone street full of quaint shops and cafes, and the magnificent York Minster, one of the greatest Gothic churches in Northern Europe. For an immersive experience in Viking history, visit the Jorvik Viking Centre. Alternatively, take a tour of the National Railway Museum, which has an excellent collection of antique locomotives. York's historic city walls and Guildhall are two more examples of its rich past. The city's rich cultural landscape, with several festivals, theaters, and galleries, ensures there's always something to see and do. York is a rewarding day trip destination because of its unique combination of historical significance and vibrant atmosphere.

Lake District

Although significantly further out, the Lake District is a lovely national park roughly two hours from Manchester by vehicle or train, offering some of the most spectacular natural landscapes in the UK. The Lake District, with its placid lakes, untamed mountains, and quaint towns, is ideal for people looking for quiet getaways and outdoor experiences. Hiking, boating, cycling, and touring charming towns such as Keswick, Ambleside, and Windermere are popular pastimes. The Beatrix Potter Gallery in Hawkshead and Dove Cottage, the poet William Wordsworth's residence, honour the area's literary ties. The Lake District provides a wide variety of experiences that suit all interests and fitness levels, whether you are taking a leisurely boat trip on Lake Windermere or climbing Scafell Pike, the highest peak in England.

Chester Zoo

Chester Zoo, an ideal day trip destination for families and animal enthusiasts, is roughly an hour's drive or train ride from Manchester. Chester Zoo is home to nearly 21,000 animals from more than 500 species, making it one of the biggest and most well-known zoos in the UK. With immersive exhibits that mimic natural environments and offer enlightening information about wildlife preservation, the zoo is dedicated to conservation and education. The vast African Savanna, the Gorilla Rainforest, and the Chimpanzee Forest are among the highlights. Chester Zoo provides visitors of all ages with an engaging and educational experience through interactive encounters, animal performances, and educational talks.

Manchester is ideally situated to explore some of the most fascinating locations in Northern England. These suggested day trips offer a variety of experiences to enhance your vacation, whether you are drawn to the natural beauty of the Peak District and Lake District, the rich history of Chester and York, the vibrant culture of Liverpool, or the amazing wildlife of Chester Zoo. Make the most of your stay in and around Manchester by using the current information, gorgeous images, and thorough maps in this guide to organise your excursions with confidence. Take advantage of the chance to wander outside the city limits and experience the distinct allure and splendour that every location presents, crafting priceless memories during your Manchester journey in 2024 and beyond.

Packing Tips for Manchester

Carefully preparing for a vacation to Manchester can guarantee that you arrive at your destination feeling relaxed and prepared to take advantage of everything this energetic city has to offer. With Manchester's varied activities, dynamic climate, and busy urban setting, having the appropriate essentials can really make a difference. In-depth packing guidance, helpful suggestions, and the most recent information can all be found in this section of your indispensable travel companion, which will help you prepare wisely for your Manchester trip in 2024 and beyond.

Recognise the Weather in Manchester
Manchester is well known for its erratic weather, which is marked by a lot of rain and yearly temperature fluctuations. It is important to bring adaptable clothing that can change with the weather if you want to stay comfortable and organised.
- **Layered Clothing**: It is important to layer because Manchester's weather can change quickly. Bring t-shirts, long-sleeve shirts, and lightweight sweaters that are simple to add or remove as needed.
- **Jacket Waterproof**: It is imperative to have a premium waterproof or water-resistant garment. In order to stay dry during unexpected showers, look for one with a hood.

- **Umbrella**: When it rains in the city, a lightweight, durable umbrella is a useful addition that does not take up much room in your suitcase.

Cosy Sneakers

Whether you are strolling in the parks, visiting museums, or meandering through old neighbourhoods, exploring Manchester frequently requires a lot of walking. Comfortable footwear is an essential to ensure you can enjoy your day without discomfort.

- **Walking Shoes**: Make an investment in a supportive, comfy pair of trainers or walking shoes. When it rains, choose waterproof shoes to keep your feet dry.
- **Casual Boots**: These fashionable yet useful boots go well with a variety of ensembles and offer the support you need for extended strolls.

Seasonal Necessities

Manchester experiences distinct seasons, each requiring special goods to keep you comfortable and prepared.

- **Summer**: Breathable fabrics, shorts, and skirts are great choices for light apparel. Remember to pack sunscreen, a hat, and sunglasses to protect yourself from the occasional sunny day.

- **Cold**: Bring warm clothing, such as thermals, sweaters, a thick coat, beanie, gloves, and scarves. Winters in Manchester may be cold and wet, so staying warm is crucial.

Travel Records and Requirements

A seamless vacation depends on having all the travel paperwork and basics in order.

- **Visas and Passports**: Verify that your visa is valid for a minimum of six months beyond the date of your intended departure. Check if you require a visa to enter the UK and get one in advance if needed.

- **Travel Insurance**: To cover unforeseen circumstances like medical emergencies, trip cancellations, or lost possessions, comprehensive travel insurance is strongly advised.
- **Copies of Vital Records**: Maintain physical and digital copies of your travel insurance, passport, visas, and critical contacts apart from the originals.

Sanitation and Health

A nice travel experience depends on maintaining your health and cleanliness.

- **Medications**: Bring a copy of the prescription for any prescription drugs you require. Bringing a modest first aid kit with necessary items like bandages, painkillers, and antiseptic wipes is also a smart idea.
- **Toilets**: Bring travel-sized amenities, such as toothpaste, shampoo, conditioner, and toothbrush. Make sure you have adequate skincare or grooming supplies with you for the duration of your trip.

Technology and Gadgets

Technology and gadgets are essential for travelling since they keep you connected and powered up.

- **Mobile phone and power source:** For communication, navigation, and accessing travel apps, your smartphone is an essential tool. Remember to carry a dependable charger.

- **Power Source:** It is necessary to pack a proper power adaptor to charge your electronics because the UK utilises Type G electrical outlets.

- **Transportable Power Source:** Your gadgets will remain charged all day with a portable battery pack, especially if you go on lengthy excursions.

Useful Accessory

A few items can improve the functionality and convenience of your travels and increase the enjoyment of your stay.

- **Reusable Bottle of Water:** It is crucial to stay hydrated, and using reusable water bottles cuts down on plastic waste. Water refill facilities are available in a lot of Manchester public spaces.

- **Daypack**: When touring the city, a lightweight daypack is helpful for holding your necessities. Select one with several sections for improved organisation.

- **Maps and Travel Guide**: A printed travel guide or map can be a useful backup even if digital maps and apps are invaluable especially in places with spotty internet access.

Room for Memorabilia

Manchester has lots of places to buy original presents and souvenirs. Make sure your luggage has enough room, or think about bringing a collapsable suitcase for the return journey.

- **Extra Luggage Space**: Make sure your suitcase has enough space for mementos such as apparel, crafts, or artisanal foods.

- **Collapsible Tote**: To carry extra stuff without overpacking, a lightweight, foldable tote bag might be a handy addition.

Last Minute Packing Advice

- **Light Travel:** Try to carry as little as possible in order to save bulk and weight. The effective public transport system in Manchester makes it simple to move around with your possessions.

- **Verify the baggage policies of the airline:** Familiarize yourself with your airline's baggage restrictions regarding size, weight, and carry-on allowances to prevent any surprises at the airport.

- **Climatic Update:** Check Manchester's weather prediction before you depart in case you need to make last-minute changes to your packing list.

Making meticulous travel preparations will guarantee that you are ready for Manchester's varied activities and dramatic weather. You can concentrate on enjoying your trip and making the most of your stay in this fascinating and culturally diverse city if you heed these packing suggestions. Utilize the up-to-date information, practical tips, and precise maps in this guide to pack sensibly and start on a memorable Manchester journey in 2024 and beyond. With confidence, embrace the spirit of discovery, knowing that you are up to the challenges Manchester has in store for you.

Printed in Great Britain
by Amazon